GO FORWARD

Your Personal Guide to Move From Stuck
to Abundance

Keshawna Salmon-Ferguson

DAYELight
PUBLISHERS

ISBN: 978-1-958443-52-1 (paperback)

Scripture quotations marked "KJV" are taken from the Holy Bible,
King James Version (Public Domain).

Scripture quotations marked (NIV) are taken from the Holy Bible, New
International Version®, NIV®. Copyright © 1973, 1978, 1984 by
Biblica, Inc.™ Used by permission of Zondervan. All rights reserved
worldwide.

Scripture quotations marked (NLT) are taken from the Holy Bible,
New Living Translation, copyright © 1996, 2004, 2007 by Tyndale
House Foundation. Used by permission of Tyndale House Publishers,
Inc., Carol Stream, Illinois 60188. All rights reserved.

Scripture quotations marked "ESV" are from the ESV Bible® (The
Holy Bible, English Standard Version®), copyright © 2001 by
Crossway Bibles, a publishing ministry of Good News Publishers. Used
by permission. All rights reserved.

This book is dedicated to my children,
Kristen and Shawn.
Always do the best you can with what you have.

Contents

PREFACE

I had just concluded my first sermon at a National Convocation of the Bethel United Church of Jesus Christ (Apostolic) in Jamaica. My husband's first words to me were, "Write the book!"

As I submit to God working through my husband, this book is the result of that directive.

Writing is something I had long dreamed of but had not yet accomplished. Interestingly, I had just preached about working for God. My husband's words reminded me that writing and putting words into the hands of persons that will give guidance for action is part of my work. It is an area in which I needed to advance and get on with.

Thanks, Trevor, for the inspiration.

INTRODUCTION

A s I write this book, we are in the midst of the COVID-19 pandemic. All over the world people's lives have been severely affected as we adjust to new protocols set by the World Health Organization (WHO) and the government of respective countries. These are aimed at limiting the spread of the severe acute respiratory syndrome coronavirus 2 (SARS-COV-2 virus) and, ultimately, saving lives.

The adjustments for many have been drastic, having to adhere to social/physical distancing guidelines, work from home protocols, wearing of masks, travel restrictions, and completing most tasks, including schooling online, among other things. The impact on spiritual activities has been no less. Gone are the days when dozens and hundreds of participants could gather for a church service. Where allowed, persons must take turns to attend face-to-face/in-person church services, as numbers for gatherings have been restricted. Many have been robbed of the opportunity to get closure after losing a loved one with the restrictions on funeral services. The new modus operandi is services and meetings via Zoom, YouTube, or other online platforms.

For many, the unexpected changes associated with the pandemic have left them feeling hopeless, helpless, and having no direction as they struggle to make sense of life with COVID-19. Life in many ways has come to a standstill. Many previous churchgoers have not attended a church service in many months, online or in-person. Several programs have not been offered, and many have stopped serving as they used to. It is within this context that the Lord gave presiding Bishop Devon C. Brown of the Bethel United Church of Jesus Christ (Apostolic) in Jamaica and the Caribbean a word to challenge His people. The word was *"Go Forward...Get On With It!"*

Indeed, life must continue despite COVID-19 or any other situation that comes to challenge us in the various spheres. Truth be told, while COVID-19 has had its impact, there are many things that we have not been diligent in attending to prior to COVID-19, and that have been exacerbated by the pandemic. There are ideas that have not been pursued, areas of interest that lie neglected, and things to be done that have been left undone.

An honest reflection will lead to identifying areas for advancement and growth in our lives. While we should never discount our past accomplishments nor diminish the importance of current pursuits, stagnation should never be accepted. There are areas in which we need to move forward, and some other things that we need to get on with for greater effectiveness and to fulfill purpose.

I have been moved by an observation as I interact with people in various contexts. I realize that many people are merely enduring; they are not enjoying life. Some people are just doing what they can to survive and not thriving. Similarly, others are just keeping their head above the waters, literally taking each day as it comes with no hope or aspiration for the future. Many are going through the motion as they awake each day, doing only what they must.

Various situations and circumstances have led people to be in a place where they are existing but not truly living; breathing, but not alive. This is not in keeping with the abundant life I believe we are meant to experience. It is a life abounding in joy, peace, love, and other virtues that make your life meaningful and fulfilled.

This state of less-than-abundant living is very concerning, especially when one looks at the lives of some Christians. Christ admonishes in the Scriptures in John 10:10 that, *"I am come that they might have life, and that they might have it more abundantly" (KJV).* This suggests that living in a way that you experience satisfaction and fulfilment is something to be achieved. Thus, persons not having such experience of abundance have something yet to attain. They need to go forward.

This book has been written with many people in mind—people who need to go forward. If you need to move beyond where you currently are in some area of life to be at a better place emotionally, intellectually, socially, financially, physically, in relationships, in your spiritual walk, or any other aspect, this book was written with you in mind. If there is an area in which you need to achieve something more, this book was meant for you. If you know anyone you could help advance in his or her life, this book was also meant for you.

It is my hope that insights will be gained from the pages of this book that will form the basis for action that will lead to individuals living more satisfying, fulfilling, and, ultimately, more abundant lives. The stark reality is that while we have come a far way as individuals and institutions, there is yet more to be accomplished. There is still work to be done if another level is to be attained. We must go forward. For some, it is the start of a journey; for others, it is continuing a journey. Whatever stage you are in, there is a need to go forward.

If this is your desire, journey with me through the pages of this book to understand some God-inspired thoughts on the matter. You can choose to read the entire book or zero in on sections of interest. However you decide to engage with the material in this volume, I pray that your life will be transformed by a word from God to your spirit and that you will find the discipline to take the necessary action to *Go Forward. Be blessed.*

The book is framed around questions that you might ask as you seek to understand how to move forward. The five essential questions are what, how, who, when, and why? In which of these areas are your questions about going forward focused? I believe that you will find useful answers in this volume to guide you in taking your next steps as you *Go Forward.*

There are also many questions embedded within each chapter. These are geared towards facilitating real-time reflection on the concepts presented. You can jot down your thoughts in the note pages at the end of each chapter as you are challenged to take action.

WHAT?

CHAPTER 1

WHAT DOES IT MEAN TO GO FORWARD?

Several things are implied by these two words: *go forward*. Firstly, the word *go* is an imperative, that is, a word used to give a command and order. You are being advised to take a particular action. In this case, the action being ordered is that of movement from one place to another. According to the Cambridge Dictionary, one definition of *go* is to travel or move to another place.

Inherent in this definition is the suggestion that you are at a particular position or place; however, there is reason to move to another. Some action is required. To go is a verb. It requires doing something—moving.

It is important to note that not any movement is associated with going. You must leave from one place and move to another to go. This describes locomotion. Thus, the lifting of the arm, which can be described as movement, does not result in you *going*, at least, not in the literal sense of the word. When you *go*, the entire body is taken to another place. You advance. When you advance, progress is made.

This being considered, you should not confuse doing with going. Activity or movement in some part of the body—doing something—if it does not result in you being taken to a different place, if advancement is not made, the directive to *go* is not fulfilled. Said another way, because you are doing something, it does not mean you are going anywhere.

You, for example, can run in place for thirty minutes. Yes, it would provide some workout with all the movement involved. If, however, you should have gone to the park and back in the thirty minutes, with all the movement, you did not go. Not learning to go up and down those hills on the way to and from the park will cost you when the 5K race/walk comes around.

As you reflect on this point, it is important to consider the activities you are engaged in and all the things you do in various aspects of your life. To what extent have they facilitated movement from one place or position to another? In what way are you advancing, making progress, developing, or improving from being involved in them? Are you *going* somewhere or are you just marking time? If the latter for you is true, the directive is to *go*. You need to begin to do something that is going to take you beyond where you presently are. You need to move.

> *Don't confuse doing with advancing. Because one is doing something, it does not mean one is going anywhere.*

Moving

The physical process of movement involves several elements. The brain works in conjunction with the muscles, which work with the bones in the skeletal system to produce movement. When the need or desire to move is registered in the brain, it sends signals via the nervous system, which includes the spinal cords and nerves, to the muscles. This causes the muscles to contract. When muscles contract, they pull on bones through tendons, and bones pull on each other through ligaments, causing them to bend at joints, resulting in movement.

Muscles work in pairs of flexors and extensors in the process of movement. Flexor muscles contract to bend a limb at a joint. The flexor muscles then relax, and extensor muscles contract to extend or straighten the limb at the same joint.

Contraction of the muscles in the leg is the main way we move our feet to stand, walk, run, or jog. Other muscles are also involved in the process of locomotion, including those in the thighs, knees, and feet.

Besides muscles directly associated with the feet, other areas of the body are involved in locomotion. Walking is thus considered a full-body exercise. While the legs are working, the arms need to swing, and the core of the body works to stabilize you while you are moving.

As with movement that results in locomotion, the act of *going* involves a process. This process begins with a need or desire registered in the brain to move. This need or desire then triggers actions in other parts of the body that ultimately result in movement. This means that locomotion will not occur if the brain does not receive and process the stimulus to move from one place to another. Locomotion might also not occur if there is some malfunction in parts of the system involved in movement such as the legs.

I contend that the greater of the two issues is the brain not receiving the stimulus to trigger action to move the body. The brain is the body's operation center. If a signal does not reach the brain, it cannot direct the rest of the body to act. The brain will only initiate movement if it is activated by some stimulus to do so. Otherwise, it will keep the body doing other voluntary and involuntary actions for which signals were received.

From a pragmatic perspective, this brings into question the extent to which the need for movement, that is, the need to *go,* is registered in your brain to spur related actions. As you look around and acknowledge areas where movement and changes are necessary but are not being undertaken in individual lives and institutions, it suggests that it might not yet be registered in the brain that the current position is not optimal and therefore movement to another place is required. This disconnect can cause people to do the same thing repeatedly and expect better or different results. This could result from mindlessness.

When you are mindless, you are not paying attention or giving much thought to the things and situations in the environment. On the other hand, the mindful person is more inclined to be aware and attend to stimuli that prompt adjustment and action. On a point of reflection, how mindless or mindful are you about the situations in your area of influence that require movement and that should prompt you to go?

What are the things staring you in the face that you have not seen? What has been blasting in your ears, yet you have not heard? What pungent aroma has been in the air around you, yet you have not detected the odor? What has been rubbing you hard, yet you have not detected the touch? So many things that prompt movement have not registered in the brain—they are nowhere in the conscious mind.

> *Pay attention!*
> *Pay attention so you do not miss cues for action.*
> *Pay attention to sights, sounds, feelings, thoughts, experiences, and anything that provides cues for movement.*

To be conscious of triggers that testify of the need for movement, you must pay attention. Pay attention so as not to miss cues for action. Pay attention to identify cues that might have been previously missed. Pay attention to sights, sounds, feelings, thoughts, experiences, and anything that provides cues for movement that need to be registered in consciousness. Pay attention.

Are you seeing things around you, in organizations, or people you are associated with that need to be changed? Is there a need for movement in some areas? Are you concerned that the relevant persons are not taking action that might be quite obvious to you? It is possible that there is an absence of conscious awareness about the matter. Yes, it could be staring them in the face, yet they do not see, and blasting in their ears, yet they have not heard. Your role might be to help bring conscious awareness to the matter, as there will be no movement until that happens. Get them to pay attention as well.

Some principles in Physics are also instructive for this subject of movement. Newton's first law of motion states that a body continues in its state of rest or uniform motion in a straight line unless acted on by a resultant force. This means that matter—anything that occupies space—tends to be lazy or demonstrate what is called inertia. It resists changes in motion. This inertia makes it difficult for an object to start, stop, change direction, or accelerate.

And, oh, how true this is for humans. Many people are experiencing inertia. Some have not taken the necessary action that will move them to a better place—they have problems starting. Others are doing things that are not fruitful but keep doing so ritualistically, although doing otherwise would yield better results—they have problems stopping and changing direction. Yet others are on a path that is beneficial but could be achieving more if the pace was increased—they have problems accelerating. All these persons need to get in motion. They need to get going, go in another direction, or go faster— they all need to *go*. Do any of these describe you?

Do you need to get going in some area of your life? If there is an area of your life where not much has happened and where things need to be happening, this might be speaking to you. Is there an aspect of your life that requires you to reroute? If you are on a path that is not yielding the desired results and you need to go in another direction, this might be you. Are you heading in the right direction but need to increase your momentum—go faster? If you are not maximizing your potential, this might be you. This is a stock-taking moment. How are things adding up for you?

Another principle highlighted in the movement process is the importance of systems and processes. Just as movement does not occur by the feet alone, moving will necessitate various interrelated systems operating to facilitate this action. As you think about your situation, what are the interconnected aspects that need to be activated to facilitate movement? What are the various things that need to be functioning together? What will you need to do to ensure that the various aspects are functioning as they should to ensure movement?

Take time to reflect on your situation. Yes, take some time to understand the various elements that are important in the movement process. What are the things that need to come into play for you to move forward in that aspect of your life? Write them down. It is important to pay attention to these elements to ensure they are activated as necessary and functioning as they should. What steps will you take to get the various systems or aspects of the system functioning to ensure that you go forward? Begin acting today.

Moving Forward

So far, we have explored what it means to go. Let us now look at the other word *forward*, in the two-word command. While the word *go* speaks to action, the word *forward* gives direction to the movement. You must move from one position or place to another, but to where and in what direction?

The word *forward* speaks to the direction you are facing or traveling—the direction that is in front of you. It is moving onward to make progress. It is concerned with the future.

Go forward therefore means move into your future. Take actions that will cause you to make progress or advance from where you currently are. Achieve more. Move to a better place in your emotions, finances, relationships, health, career, leadership, pursuits, and all other aspects of your life.

The directive to proceed in a forward direction also implies that other directions of movement are possible. Indeed backwards, lateral/sideway, and circular movements are all possible. You must, therefore, take the command seriously. It is not just *go* but *go forward*.

Movement on a path that emphasizes focus on past accomplishments and achievements as well as past failures and experiences is not the desired direction. Yes, winning the last award speaks well of your past effort and work. However, spending most of your time basking in yesterday's accomplishment will not provide the necessary force to overcome the inertia associated with the high you feel from the thrill of success. Unless you build on what was previously done, there will be no future awards or rewards.

> *Don't get stuck recounting the experiences of yesterday that you miss out on other experiences that will count for more tomorrow.*

Similarly, spending time to rehash and brood over negative events and failures of the past depletes the energy necessary to overcome the inertia to make investments in things that will have future positive outcomes. Don't get stuck recounting the experiences of yesterday that you miss out on other experiences that will count for more tomorrow.

In his book, *The Power of Your Potential*, John Maxwell sheds some light on how highs and lows can control our lives and limit growth, and, by extension, movement. He gave advice on how not to let the negatives take one too low or the positives take one too high

Maxwell said, "Successes have a tendency to make us complacent. We start to assume that everything will automatically stay good, so we are tempted to rest on our laurels and try to protect what we have. We can begin to feel entitled, lose perspective, and stop working hard. In the end, both highs and lows have the ability to rob us of reality and limit our activity."[1]

To deal with this, Maxwell suggests limiting the impact of highs and lows by allowing oneself a specific period or amount of time to bask in the high or wallow in the low. A time limit of twenty-four hours is recommended after the occurrence of high or low experiences to return to a level of emotional stability. It is important to take action and get back on track. Maxwell reminds readers that "Yesterday's success won't bring us tomorrow's success. Today's work does."[2]

How many twenty-four hours have you spent walking in the past, thinking about all the things that have happened and

---

[1] Maxwell, J. (2018). *The power of your potential: How to breakthrough your limits.* Hachette Book Group. (page 33).

[2] Maxwell, J. (2018). *The power of your potential: How to breakthrough your limits.* Hachette Book Group. (page 34).

not happened that should have happened, and how they were good or bad, how you can't manage, how hard things have been, or even how great things are? I suspect many persons are over the one-day limit and maybe have gone days, weeks, months, and even years beyond. It is time to make an about-turn and head in the opposite direction. *Go forward.*

Some persons have gone so far back in their thinking and behaviours that psychologists would describe them as having regressed. Regression is a defense mechanism, a mental process used to reach compromise solutions to conflicts that one is unable to resolve in the mind. Regression involves a return to earlier stages of development rather than handling impulses more adaptively. It is usually exhibited in the return to less mature or more childish ideas and behaviours in response to situations. It can also involve a fixation on reliving earlier times. To go forward, regressive behaviors need to be brought into the realm of consciousness, acknowledged, and replaced with more beneficial behaviors. Some of these more useful behaviours will be discussed later in the book.

There are times when going backward can be useful in the context of making redress or dealing with unresolved issues; however, ultimately, the purpose of dealing with situations from the past is with the aim of moving forward. Going backward in such contexts are temporary actions required to make one better

> *Going forward with intentionality might mean making decisions to choose paths that are unfamiliar, but that will stretch you. It will require a mindset to deal with the uncomfortable.*

24

equipped to move forward. I think of it as going out into the cold, but you realize that you have left your jacket. You return inside the house just to pick up the jacket and immediately go back through the door and continue on your forward journey. If you need to go back, make this a temporary state to immediately deal with something that needs to be attended to in order to be in a better place to move forward. Going backward should never be a lasting state. Don't go back into the house and settle down into the coziness of a familiar space. Grab your coat and head back through the door. You are going forward.

Looking now at lateral movement, one example that comes to mind is changing job positions. When you take on a new job that is at the same career level as the previous or current job, albeit with different duties, this is considered a sideways or lateral move. Yes, there are times when a lateral move can be powerful, but it may not be the correct move if you should be moving forward.

Taking a position at a similar level in another department at the same company or another institution may be helpful if it, for example, gives more flexibility in time to attend to children. In fact, while a lateral move career-wise, it could be a powerful forward move when it comes to focusing on what matters. The time spent nurturing children is always a useful investment.

On the other hand, moving to another department at a similar position might not be the right move if you dream of doing and becoming more, and your principles and values are no longer in sync with the company's. Hiding in another department is just a temporary fix. Your inner longing for significance will likely remain unresolved as you will not be stretched or pushed to the next level where your true potential will be realized. You need to get on with it! Go forward.

John Maxwell calls this "intentional living." It is a life that brings daily satisfaction and continual rewards as one works to make a difference, small or great. It is about becoming more proactive in making your life matter and stepping into your own story. Yes, it is about taking action that leads to the fulfilment of purpose and living a life of significance.

If you are going to move forward into your future, a lateral move might not do. Choosing an alternate path because it seems easier or is closest to what you are used to and will keep you in your comfort zone is not the way to maximize your potential. It is not the way to go forward. Making such a move could, in fact, be more detrimental in the long term as it would not have been an intentional action.

Maxwell says, if "you never act with intentionality, you're actually likely to become more frustrated and less fulfilled because your desire for positive change may increase, but lack of results will leave you frustrated." "If you're going to grow," he says, "you have to be intentional."[3]

Going forward with intentionality might mean making decisions to choose paths that are unfamiliar, but that will stretch you. It will require a mindset to deal with the uncomfortable. It will also involve doing new things that tap

---

[3] Maxwell, J. C. (2015). *Intentional living: Choosing a life that matters.* Center Street. (page 31).

into your true purpose—no more unnecessary lateral movement.

I had an experience a few years ago that can be related to circular movement. It is certainly an experience that I will never forget.

In May 2018, my teenage daughter and I attended the Calabash International Literary Festival held in Treasure Beach, St. Elizabeth in Jamaica. Due to the popularity of the festival, we were not able to find lodging in the parish where the event was being staged, and so had to stay in Mandeville, a town nearby.

Sometime after midnight on the Friday of the event, we journeyed from Treasure Beach to Mandeville. While I had a general idea of the directions, I was not familiar with all the roads and turns and, therefore, needed the assistance of a Global Positioning System (GPS) to find my way. We reached a point where we needed to get to Spur Tree, a winding road with a steep incline. This is where the GPS had us going in circles.

The area is a rural setting with some footpaths and ill-defined roads in addition to the main road. The area was also not well-lit and had few road signs. Mapping of such an area would have been incomplete, and therefore the GPS detected paths that were categorized as roads but would only allow human and animal traffic. In this instance, the GPS kept directing me to drive along a route that appeared to be the shortest path but was not for vehicular traffic.

I initially took the route suggested by the GPS. However, upon realizing that it was leading me to a path where it was not possible to drive, I tried going in another direction. After driving for a while, it occurred to me that I kept coming back to the same place where I was minutes ago, so I had not progressed. It struck me that every time I tried to go in a direction away from the path that the GPS was originally sending me, because I kept relying on the GPS, it kept rerouting me, not to a different path, but to the route it ultimately wanted me to take.

> *Beware of going around in circles— moving but going nowhere.*

It was now nearly 1AM. I was alone with my teenage daughter in a dark, lonely place. My husband was miles away and could not help. I had to find a way to move forward. I could not continue going around in circles—moving but going nowhere.

I recognized that I needed a new compass bearing. The GPS was not positioning me in the right direction. I had to ditch the GPS. No, I did not throw it out as I knew it would still be useful later with some updates and on more well-defined roads. I simply turned it off. I had to rely on my internal compass and God as my guide.

I kept driving in the general direction that I believed would take me toward Spur Tree. I anticipated that soon enough, I would find something that would help me to find the correct path that I should be on. Fortunately, as I had hoped, I came upon another motorist who willingly detoured from his route and drove with me to the point where I could clearly determine the route to my destination. I kept going forward. I made it to my destination.

How many people are in the position that I was in; going around in circles, moving but going nowhere—making some strides that you think are putting you on a forward path, but keep following a GPS that keeps pulling you back to the same place you thought you had left?

Think of spinning an object on a string. The object will never fly off—move forward—once it remains on the string. The centrifugal force associated with the pull of the string will always have it going in circles. For the object to move forward the connection to the string that has it going in loops has to be cut.

Like I did, you need to beware of going around in circles—moving but going nowhere. If you are in such a position, a new positioning system is required. Like that object, you will need to cut the tie to the thing that has you going around in circles.

What positioning system are you relying on? Is it your negative thoughts? Is it your unrealistic expectations? Is it the discouraging words and ideas of others? Is it your feeling of low self-worth and low self-esteem? Is it your lack of confidence? What keeps pulling you towards that circular path where you are doing things, but not much is achieved? Is it your fear? Is it your lack of development in some important area? What is holding you back? You need to ditch that GPS and cut that string. It is time to go forward.

Reflections and Notes

What are your takeaways from this chapter? What will you pay attention to, and what actions will you take?

_____

_____

_____

_____

_____

_____

_____

_____

_____

_____

_____

_____

_____

_____

_____

_____

_____

_____

_____

_____

_____

_____

_____

_____

_____

_____

_____

_____

_____

_____

_____

_____

_____

_____

_____

_____

_____

_____

_____

CHAPTER 2

WHAT DO I NEED TO GO FORWARD?

As I write this chapter, I am sitting on the deck of the Adventure of the Seas, watching as the large vessel which is the size of a hotel moves gracefully along the calm blue waters of the Atlantic Ocean. As I observed the distinct ripples left by the ship as it sailed through the waters, I wondered what it takes for this ship to move forward.

Certainly, the fee paid by the more than three thousand passengers for their getaway cruise is a great propelling force. However, I concluded that that was not enough to ensure that the ship moved forward. Everyone aboard at the Cape Liberty Cruise Port was a necessary but insufficient condition to ensure forward movement. It requires more than the allure of the seas for the ship to move forward.

Like other marine transportation, the cruise ship has a built-in system responsible for providing the force needed to create forward movement. The Adventure of the Seas is equipped with a diesel-electric power station. Without this

---

internal mechanism, the journey from Cape Liberty to Halifax via the Atlantic Ocean would be wishful thinking.

Various sea vessels will have different marine propulsion systems, including diesel, wind, and gas turbines on larger boats and ships, and paddles and sails on smaller boats. Similarly, going forward in the air or on land doesn't just happen. The airplane, helicopter, hot air balloon, or even a kite each has a propulsion system. The car, tractor, motorcycle, cart, and wagons are either motor-powered or manually propelled. Forward movement doesn't just happen. There is always a force responsible for movement.

An applied force that overcomes static friction is needed to produce motion. That applied force can be produced through various means. For example, wind moving around an object causing some change in pressure can result in the object moving forward. Internal combustion produced by burning fuel in an engine can produce enough force to push the object forward. Similarly, manual pushing or pulling of an object can result in an object moving away from or in the direction of the driving force. Something must act on the object in every instance to get it moving. What is that force required to move you forward?

Personalities and Driving Forces

As transportation is varied, so are humans. Similarly, different types of forces are required to get different people moving. Such differences are often related to differences in personality.

The American Psychological Association defines personality as individual differences in characteristic patterns of thinking, feeling, and behaving.[4] The personality is generally depicted as traits. These are relatively stable, consistent, and enduring internal characteristics that are inferred from a pattern of behaviors, attitudes, and habits in an individual. Said another way, a personality trait is an enduring personality characteristic that describes or determines an individual's behavior across a range of situations.[5] It is the tendency to think, feel, and act in a certain way across various situations over time.

There are a variety of theories of personality that identify various personality traits. Many personality tests have also been developed based on such theories to identify the personality traits that form part of one's identity. While personality traits are not deterministic, meaning that they cannot guarantee how a person will behave under all circumstances, traits give a fair idea of how persons will generally operate. An understanding of various personality traits is therefore useful to further understand what are possible forces that could serve as driving factors to propel one forward.

One personality model and related assessment that I have come to appreciate, which has been useful in my life and work, is the DISC Personality Profile. DISC is an acronym that represents the four main personality traits or behavioral styles

---

[4] https://www.apa.org/topics/personality

[5] APA Dictionary of Psychology https://dictionary.apa.org/personality-trait

in the DISC model of human behaviour, namely: *Dominant, Inspiring, Supportive, and Cautious.*[6]

The foundations for the DISC model are two basic drives: the motor (pace) drive and the compass (priority) drive.[7] With respect to pace, some people are more outgoing or faster-paced, while others are more reserved or slower-paced. People with an outgoing drive tend to move, talk, and/or decide on things fast. On the other hand, people who are reserved tend to speak more slowly and softly and generally prefer to consider things carefully and thoroughly before deciding. While most people will exhibit a bit of both reserved or outgoing traits depending on the situation, they will tend to exhibit more of one trait or the other, even if slightly more.

As it regards priority, some persons are more task-oriented or focused, while others tend to have a more people-oriented or focused perspective. People who are more task-oriented or focused tend to focus more on logic, data, results, and projects. People who have more of a people orientation tend to focus on experiences, feelings, relationships, and interactions. As with the motor drive paradigm, while people will exhibit a blend of both the task-oriented and the people-oriented drive depending on the situation, people tend to exhibit more of one trait over the other at their core.

---

[6] Retrieved from https://discpersonalitytesting.com/blog/what-is-the-disc-model/

[7] More information on these drives can be found on a website dedicated to the DISC method by the Kevin Eikenberry Group
https://discpersonalitytesting.com/blog/what-is-the-disc-model/

Based on the information presented so far, how would you describe yourself? On the dimension of motor drive, or that power unit inside of you that generates motion, are you more outgoing and faster paced or more reserved and slower paced? On the dimension of compass drive, or that thing on the inside that indicates direction, do you give greater priority to task-oriented or people-oriented matters? The combination of your orientation on both dimensions represents a behavior style and gives an indication of the type of forces that drive you.

If you are more of a task-oriented person, how many of the activities that you undertake daily require you to be more focused on aspects of a task rather than people-related aspects? To what extent is the opposite true for you if you are more people-oriented? Is there a reasonable balance in line with your preference?

Where are you with respect to the balance between being reserved and outgoing? To what extent are your daily activities in sync with your innate inclinations? Might you need to consider some adjustments that align you with your preferred pace? What might you need to do to create greater balance in

> *Know yourself and be true to yourself. Don't get stuck doing something that is wrong for your personality type.*

favour of your innate personality style? This could be a driving force that moves you forward in the direction of your true personality type.

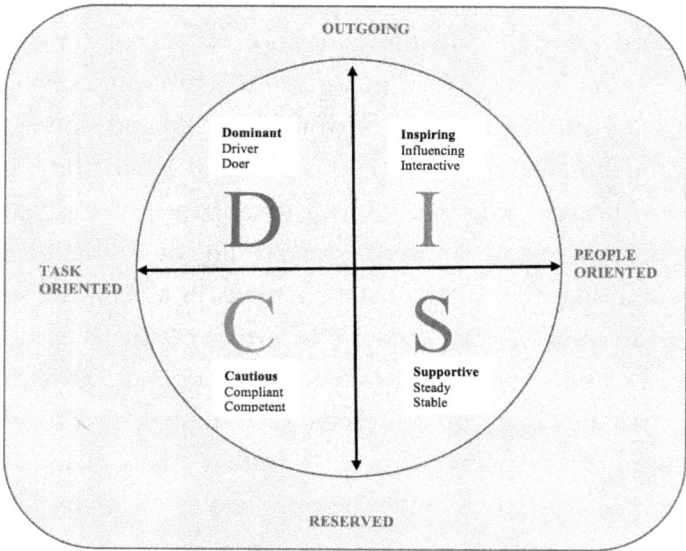

Figure 1. The DISC model of human behavior.

The DISC model of human behavior is represented by Figure 1. Each main personality/behavioral style is represented in a quadrant. You would likely fall in the "D" quadrant with people who often exhibit ***dominant*** and ***direct*** behaviours if you are more outgoing and task-oriented. They usually focus on results, problem-solving, and the bottom line. They also tend to be decisive, are extraordinarily goal-oriented and competitive, and tend to be risk-takers and self-starters. People with high D personality type like to be in positions of authority or do things on their own terms. They have high ego strength, which can be perceived as confidence or pride.

On the other hand, if you are outgoing but more people-oriented than task-oriented in your approach, you would fall in the "I" quadrant with persons described as *inspiring* and *interactive*. People in this category are usually focused on interacting with people, having fun, and/or creating excitement. They are enthusiastic and not afraid to be the centre of attention. People with the I personality style function best when they are around other people.

If you have reserved and people-oriented traits, you would more likely fall in the "S" quadrant with others described as *supportive* and *steady.* People in the S quadrant usually focus on preserving relationships and creating or maintaining peace and harmony. People with strong S personalities tend to seek routine, predictability, and safety in their daily lives. S personalities can also be possessive of loved ones.

Finally, if you have reserved and task-oriented traits, you would likely be in the "C" quadrant with others described as *cautious* and *careful.* These people usually focus on facts, rules, and correctness. People with strong C personalities tend to think logically, analytically, and systematically and are excellent at problem-solving and creative thinking. They are described as perfectionists who hold very high standards for themselves and others. This, however, can result in them being overly critical.

It is important to note that while most persons tend to have a dominant behaviour style as described by one of the four categories outlined, it is possible to have at least one secondary DISC type, which is also high. The secondary type supports and influences the predominant type in the style blend. The various combinations of style types help to understand the variability in people and the different things that drive them.

The DISC Insights by PeopleKeys suggest that people with a high D personality style are motivated by new challenges, setting, and achieving goals, and seeing tangible results. They appreciate verbal recognition and rewards and enjoy taking risks and making decisions. [8] If you have a predominant D personality style, what new challenge could you take on or new goal could you set that would take you out of the routine in which you might have settled? In what areas do you desire to gain additional recognition and awards that could be explored? What new calculated risk could you take on that has the possibility of untold positive rewards? What could you do that gives you more personal freedom and leads to advancement opportunities? What project could you undertake that produces more physical, trackable, or tangible results? What new competition could you become involved in? On the other hand, might there be a need to check one's ego to improve communication and relationships with others? You could tap into these areas, which can serve as driving forces to move you forward.

According to PeopleKeys, the high I personality tends to be motivated by other's approval, praise, popularity, or acceptance. Persons with this personality style enjoy freedom from too many rules or regulations and gravitate towards friendly and fun environments. They thrive when they can be the talker, presenter, rapport builder, or have high influence in

---

[8] Retrieved from https://discinsights.com/personality-style-d

teams but would need others to handle the details.[9] Suppose you have a predominantly I personality style. Do you find yourself miserable doing jobs or tasks that primarily require you to work alone or that are more task-oriented than people-focused? What new project could you become involved in that would see you collaborating or interacting more with others? In what ways could you restructure tasks and activities to include more fun, or how could you include more fun in your life? Since you are so greatly affected by your environment, do you need to change it to one that is friendlier? What could you improve on or initiate that would be noteworthy? On the other hand, might the need for acceptance and praise from others lead you to take actions that are not in your best interest, such that the desire for approval needs to be tempered? How can you tap into the characteristics of the strong I personality to serve as a driving force to move you forward?

People with strong S personality styles are motivated by safety and security. They are driven to avoid conflict and to create harmonious environments with advanced listening skills that make them effective mediators. They really care about being appreciated primarily for their loyalty and dependability.[10] If you have a high S personality, it is worth evaluating where you are and what you are doing to see how comfortable you are in the environment in which you operate. Is it chaotic and unpredictable, or are things systematic and organized? Are you in a situation where you are constantly

---

[9] Retrieved from https://discinsights.com/personality-style-i

[10] Retrieved from https://discinsights.com/personality-style-s

troubled or experiencing distress? Are there physical, emotional, or psychological threats? Are you being appreciated for your contributions? The uneasy feelings could be strong signals that you need to find a situation that would give more security, associated with a greater level of peace. It might also be possible to lend your mediation skills to help bring some settling into the environment. How might you tap into the drives associated with the S personality to move you forward?

The high C personality style is motivated by information and logic. People with this personality style have exceptionally high standards and make decisions after doing much research. They like to be well-informed, thrive on doing things accurately, and desire to see tasks and projects through to completion.[11] If you have a high C personality, do you find that you are in a situation where you are frustrated by the lack of clear instructions and procedures for completing activities and are not sure exactly what is expected of you? Are you dealing with a situation where things are constantly changing but not well thought out or planned? Are you in a situation where your skills and abilities are positively acknowledged, or are you experiencing frequent negative criticism? Do you desire excellence but find that mediocrity is the order of the day in the context in which you operate? The characteristics of that strong C personality might just be indicating that where you are is not where you should be. Could it be that you need to step out and do something else or create something that will meet the high standards you desire? How might you tap into

---

[11] Retrieved from https://discinsights.com/personality-style-c

the traits and respond to the drives associated with your high C personality type?

Don't get stuck doing something that is wrong for your personality type. You can be in a situation where you are trying to fit into the mold of someone with another personality type. Someone else might have found happiness or satisfaction with doing a particular thing in a certain way, but you are struggling to follow suit. Could it be that it does not suit your personality type, and therefore, you do not have the natural driving force that would propel you forward in that area?

It is worth understanding your basic motivations and drives and using that information in a directed way to make decisions in various aspects of your life, including your career and interactions in relationships. If at all possible, take a personality profile assessment from a reputable institution or agent to get a more in-depth understanding. This could be quite useful in your quest to move forward.

Know yourself and be true to yourself. This includes understanding what drives you internally, such as those innate traits and tendencies. However, being true to yourself means taking it a step further to accepting those inner drives and taking appropriate action to deal with them appropriately.

Passion - The Heart in the Matter

I recently had an experience that has underscored the importance of understanding your personality type, what drives you to action, and, most importantly, remaining true to who you are in order to move forward. As I sought to explore avenues for financial and personal fulfilment, I was introduced to a service in the financial advising sector. With my background in Mathematics, my strong skills as a teacher and making presentations, and my drive to succeed, it was felt that this was an avenue that I could explore and make good in. I could become a successful sales agent.

I started out quite enthusiastic, putting everything into studying for the qualifying examinations, which I passed with flying colours. I was later successful in the interview that got me a pre-contract offer. I, however, had a challenge moving much further.

Besides the various external challenges that I experienced that impacted me going forward in the area, I was not making progress because of something else. I am usually enthusiastic about whatever I am doing and will go at it with all my might, regardless of the obstacles. Something was holding me back, and I was not immediately conscious of it.

When I stopped to assess the situation, I recognized that there was an inner spark that was not lit. As I listened to the manager enthusiastically advise of all the financial gains and awards to be achieved as well as the promotions and possible positions for movement within the organization, I said yes with all my mind and intellect. This is something I was more than able to do. Others with less educational achievement than I had attained could do it, so there was no reason why I could not achieve the same feat.

My head was in it and ready to move forward, but something was missing. The key was placed in the ignition and turned enough for there to be a throttle, but the engine had not fully started. There was enough energy to get auxiliary things going but not enough to move the vehicle forward. The key needed to be turned another notch to allow a full flow of fuel to the engine for a full start. The start was delayed because the switch had not turned far enough to reach my heart.

The requirements of the area did not connect with who I am at heart. It was not in concert with my personality. From all indications, the manager recruiting me into the financial area had a high D personality style, and so strived on competition, recognition, and awards and was very concerned about the bottom-line. Undoubtedly, with such a personality, she quickly moved up the ranks, consistently qualifying for the Million Dollar Round Table, and has remained outstanding in the field.

On the other hand, I am a high C who dislikes competition but am driven by doing things of interest that I love to a certain degree of perfection. The forceful, self-promoting profile is very unlike me. It is no wonder that the sight of my name on a list being compared to other agents was disconcerting instead of motivating, especially since I had not yet made any sales. Financial advising was an area that I could work in, but it was not an area of passion. It is based on a mode of operation that is the opposite of who I truly am and therefore does not have my heart.

There is a fire that needs to be ignited in the heart that will truly move you forward. Do you find that you are at a standstill or possibly struggling to move forward in an area? Could it be that it does not have your heart? Is it that it does not match your innate personality type and is not something you have passion for?

To get that driving force to move you forward, it is important to determine what has your heart. What starts someone else's engine and keeps another person going might not work for you, if it does not match your personality style and is not what you are passionate about.

> *Know what has **your** heart. What starts someone else's engine and keeps another person going might not work for you if it does not match your personality style and passion.*

This also means that you must be careful about taking counsel from others about moving forward. Very often, such advice will come from a good place as your companion shares from his or her experience. Be sure to take relevant principles, but be careful about acting on advice or suggestions about directions to be taken in your own life if it does not connect with who you are at heart. Find *your* passion. Find what has *your* heart.

I am reminded of a young lady who graduated from a prestigious university with a degree in a business area. She was fortunate to get a placement in a reputable institution in the area that she studied. While others lauded her for her accomplishments and looked forward to her upcoming graduation, she felt that she had nothing to celebrate. She disliked the job and, more so, the area that she studied. She became depressed partly because she felt like she was in a mire out of which she could not climb, and she only saw herself sinking further.

She had gotten a degree that someone else wanted her to get, in an area that others suggested would give her a good prospect of getting a job and earning money, which sadly, she had bought into. She completed the unwanted degree, got the job, and was paid reasonably well but was miserable and felt stuck. The area that she studied and in which she was working did not have her heart. Her day was spent analyzing accounting books and documents when what she really wanted was to interact with people through various forms of creative and design arts. Based on her personality traits, the young graduate was more people-focused in approach but spent her days focused on tasks she would never find interesting. Her mind revolted against this activity that was clearly not in keeping with her personality profile and did not have her heart. The only way out of the mire was to move in the direction of her heart.

In his book *Put Your Dream to the Test,* John Maxwell shared a similar story of Arnold Schwarzenegger, whose father wanted him to become a policeman and whose mom thought he should become a carpenter. However, he found his passion in the gymnasium and went on to win many bodybuilding awards, star in many films, and become a political leader. Maxwell attributed Arnold's accomplishments to him owning his dreams. You could say that the gymnasium had Arnold's heart, not carpentry or the police force.

In the same book, John Maxwell asks persons an important ownership question: Is my dream really *my* dream? This suggests that what one is dreaming about doing might not be one's own dream but someone else's. It is important to ensure that what you desire to do is based on your own dream in order to own it. Maxwell suggests that owning your dream will fire you up, give you energy, and provide wings to your spirit. This energy becomes the driving force to make the dream possible.

Owning your dream means it has your heart. And, as Maxwell says, "Only if you own it will you be able to fulfill it."[12] This was true for me with the financial advising pursuit and was also true in earlier career pursuits.

Unlike Arnold Schwarzenegger, who figured out when he was about fourteen years old that he liked the gymnasium and so began wholeheartedly to pursue that passion, I only truly found and acknowledged what has my heart in my middle adult years. Prior to that, I was doing what my parents desired or what seemed to meet their approval. My own passions and desires were subsumed into their desires so much that I, for a long time, did not know what I truly desired. I did not know what *my* dream was.

From an early age, my love for words expressed in reading and writing was converted to doing Mathematics. In fourth grade in elementary school, at my dad's request, I was kept back from going to read and enjoy books when it was library time. During that session, I was required to stay in the classroom with my homeroom teacher and complete extra work in Mathematics while all my other classmates were in the library enjoying themselves. Not that I did not like Mathematics, but the timetabled hours would have been

---

[12] Maxwell, J. & Hoskins, R. (2021). *Change your world: How anyone, anywhere can make a difference.* Harper Collins Leadership. (page 44).

enough, especially since I was not a weak student and was already doing quite well in the subject.

Later on in high school, Mathematics and the sciences were selected for me as the subjects to be pursued. My inclination towards the social sciences and desire to study in the area of the humanities was unacknowledged or dismissed. I was being directed towards a career in medicine. My interest in the mind and helping to change people's thinking was redirected to working with the brain as a medical doctor, possibly in the field of psychiatry.

As an obedient child and diligent student, I faithfully pursued the sciences, heading toward medicine. There was, however, a challenge. I encountered many struggles as I went further along in my schooling, as the sciences did not have my heart. It was grueling to complete a six-hour chemistry laboratory every Friday in my first year as an undergraduate student. I was not anxious to attend classes on a Friday morning. In fact, I rather dreaded the day. How was I then to pursue medicine when I was not coping well with a core prerequisite?

I was doing what I was required to do, but not what I really desired to do. I had told myself that I liked the sciences and was going to become a doctor because that was what was required of me. One might say I was conditioned, or it was instilled in me that medicine or engineering were the appropriate fields to pursue as a bright student, and one was selected for me. My parents wanted me to pursue medicine. Deep down, however, I did not like the sciences. There were other things I liked but was not allowed to have or pursue.

My high school Physics teacher, a Peace Corp worker, Mr. Craig Heitman, was right. He said, "Keshawna, you are not a science student." He had recognized my diligence (I worked hard and would strive for excellence in whatever I put my mind to) but also realized my shortcomings (I did not have a natural aptitude for the subject area). This meant that I had to work extra hard to achieve what would come quite easily for others because I was working in an area that was not in my strength zone.

Using Guy Hendricks' definitions in his book *The Big Leap*, the sciences represented a sub-genius zone for me. It was in the Zone of Competence, not the Zone of Excellence or Zone of Genius. Studying the sciences, therefore, did not bring me much satisfaction and did not provide much impetus to go forward in the area. I was unhappy. The sciences did not have my heart.

Fortunately, I was paying attention to my feelings. I came to the place where I openly acknowledged that my heart was not in the sciences and that medicine would not be my path to fulfilment. I did not want to disappoint my father, but I could do no less if I was going to be true to myself. I needed to find the inspiration, energy, fire, and passion to move forward with my studies in a way that was enjoyable and meaningful, even if I did not yet know where the path would lead.

At the end of the first year, I met with the Dean of the science faculty in which I was based to request a transfer to another faculty. It was interesting that after looking at my records, he asked, "What are you doing in this faculty? You should not have been here in the first place." He quickly gave me the letter to facilitate my transfer to other faculties in the University with courses closer to what spoke to my heart. After the transfer, I pursued courses across both the social sciences and humanities and have not encountered a struggle in schooling since then.

Yes, it has taken some time to fully unlearn and move away from the expectations of others and then to find and embrace who I really am at the core. That process, however, began with my move from the sciences to the social sciences and humanities in my sophomore year. The process of finding out where my heart is has given me the energy and drive to keep going forward and not remain stuck in a rut of doing what is in the heart of others.

Could it be that, like I was, you have had a challenge moving forward or have been feeling stuck because, for some time now, you have been doing or attempting to do what is another person's dream for you and not your own? To go forward, it is important to know what has your heart. What is it that matters to you? What is it that has meaning for you? What is it that holds your interest? What are you passionate about?

Follow *your* heart. That's a great propelling force to move you forward. Emphasis is placed on *your* heart. Take care to follow your heart and not someone else's. You can jumpstart your car with power from the battery of another vehicle but can only move forward on the power from your own battery after the charging process. Your battery, your heart. Go forward as you are propelled by a heart recharged, reignited, and renewed. Find and work with your passion as you go forward. To find your passion, follow your heart.

I am reminded of the words of the song by Kenny Rogers, which was lustily rendered by my graduating class at the end of high school. It says, "When you put your heart in it, it can take you anywhere." Indeed, something powerful happens when one's heart is involved in a matter.

Reflections and Notes

What are your takeaways from this chapter? Are you living true to your personality style in your work and relationships? What will you do to ensure you are following your heart?

_____

_____

_____

_____

_____

_____

_____

_____

_____

_____

_____

_____

_____
_____
_____
_____
_____
_____
_____
_____
_____
_____
_____
_____
_____
_____
_____
_____
_____
_____
_____
_____
_____
_____
_____
_____
_____
_____

HOW?

CHAPTER 3

HOW DO I MOVE FORWARD?

I previously spoke about the brain's role as well as other structures in the leg and other parts of the body that facilitate movement. Mention was made of the fact that malfunction in parts of the system could affect locomotion. Any such issue internally in the body or mind or externally in the environment that could impact movement needs to be understood and dealt with to effectively go forward.

A few questions come to mind when considering how to move forward. Can I do it on my own, or do I need help? What pace should I move at? What should I bring? How do I overcome the challenges that impact me moving forward? Are these some of the questions you had, and do others come to mind? Journey with me as I explore issues related to these questions. Let's go forward!

Having acknowledged the need to go forward, it is important to determine your current position and situation in relation to your ability to move. One of the first things one thinks about with respect to movement is the ability to move the leg. Are my legs working okay and, by extension, are the other parts of my body facilitating movement? Asked another way, can I move?

Several things can affect the ability to walk or one's gait. My friend, Kevin Powell, comes to mind when I think about gait abnormalities. Kevin was born with Arthrogryposis. This is a congenital condition that involves multiple joint contractures (stiffness), resulting in a limited range of motion at the affected joints. Joints with contractures may be unable to fully or partially extend or bend. My friend experienced contractures in his hips and legs. He was born with his legs folded and inverted and had to undergo a series of surgeries as a child to have this corrected. He has never been able to walk without support. He uses a wheelchair and crutches to get around.

> *Simply agreeing with an idea will not move you forward. Acting on the idea—taking that step—will*

In spite of his various challenges from birth, Kevin has not been left behind. At thirty-nine years old, he served as Director of Student Affairs at the University of the Commonwealth Caribbean (UCC) and later became Principal for the Jamaica Stock Exchange eCampus. He has attained a bachelor's degree and two master's degrees. He has also learned to swim, a feat which other able-bodied persons like myself have not attempted. Despite the naysayers, Kevin got married and has two beautiful girls. He is getting on with it. He is going forward.

Kevin has recognized and accepted his physical limitations. On the other hand, he has not caused the physical challenges to limit his ability to go forward physically or otherwise. He is living a life of abundance. He is quite fun-loving, always on the go, traveling to many places as he drives himself or is transported by others.

Kevin is a prime example of how one can move forward despite gait abnormalities. While the foot is the primary organ for movement, it is not the only way to get going. There are ways to move, even if one's feet are not working well. If one wants to move, a way can be found. It requires the will to do it. Where there is a will, there is a way.

Conditions for Moving Forward

Going forward begins in the mind. You must *want* to move. You must *want* to go forward. This desire propels you to take the necessary actions that result in taking steps. Decisions based on the desire to do lead to action when you follow through. This is the will to do.

You should note that the will to do includes more than a desire. Acting and moving forward will require more than accepting the charge to go forward. That mental assent has to be translated into a decision to act in a manner that will lead to the desired movement. A decision must be made. Having accepted the charge and, by extension, the need to go forward, a question to answer as you determine how to move forward is, what decision have I made about what I will do to move forward? A decision that facilitates action is necessary.

On this note, the Bible cautions readers about the fallacy of hearing and acceding to ideas without taking necessary action. James 1:22–24 says, *"But be ye doers of the word, and not hearers only, deceiving your own selves. For if any be a hearer of the word, and not a doer, he is like unto a man beholding his natural face in a glass: For he beholdeth himself, and goeth his way, and straightway forgetteth what manner of man he was." (KJV)*.

How many things have you considered to be important but about which you have done nothing? How many times have you agreed with something in a sermon or presentation that resonated well in your spirit, but it has not gone beyond being just a good word? Agreement with an idea, if not translated into a desire that leads to a decision that propels action, will not move you forward. These four elements could be considered conditions for moving forward: ADDA – Acceptance/Agreement, Desire, Decision, and Action. They form part of the will to do.

> *Don't deceive yourself by only hearing or conceiving good ideas. Otherwise, you will be stuck in the promise of the idea and not reap the benefits from implementing the idea.*

It is about coming to a resolution about a matter and making a conscious choice about the action one will take in regard to that matter. It is about volition. It is about exercising the power of conscious choice, decision, and intention, yes, exercising that power to do. It is more than thinking about something.

It is important to stop deceiving yourself by only hearing or conceiving good ideas. Until you have exercised the will to do, yes, the will to decide and act on that idea that is considered desirable, you would not have moved forward. As such, you would still be stuck in the promise of the idea and not reaping the benefits from implementing the idea. Avoid living in your head filled only with thoughts and embrace a reality based on conscious, meaningful actions. Simply agreeing with an idea will not move you forward. Acting on the idea—taking that step—will.

Dealing with Shoulds, Oughts and Musts

With the will to go forward, you also have to believe that it is possible to do so, despite limitations. This belief will direct one to get into a wheelchair and get the wheels turning if going on foot is challenging. Persons with the will to do don't get hung up on one way to get things done. Somehow, instinctively, or otherwise, they recognize that there is always the way and another way. If one way isn't working, find another way.

How often do we look for *the* way to do something and find that we get stuck when *that* way is not apparent? We have ideas about the "right" way for something to be done, and if it doesn't happen that way, we have a challenge reorienting ourselves to another way of doing it. This keeps some persons from moving forward.

Many people find it hard to look for or try another way if what is considered the right way is not working out. In the context of movement, the conventional way to move forward is by stepping out on your own without aid. There are however many who will need to move forward another way. They need to go with walkers, crutches, a wheelchair, or even be lifted in extreme instances. My friend, Kevin, is an example of someone who has found another way to move forward.

Some persons have not moved, and, by extension, are not going forward because, for them, movement should happen a particular way. They have specific ideas about what it entails to do something; if those conditions are not met, they do nothing. They have a way to move. It is as if they are saying, "If I can't walk on my own, I am not going anywhere." They have the attitude that says, "It's not working this way, the way it ought to; therefore, I can't go forward." A more useful approach would be to say, "It's not working this way, the way I expected it to. There has got to be another way to go forward, and I will find it."

Psychologist Albert Ellis might describe such persons as having a problem with "musterbation." This refers to people who believe they MUST live by some absolute and often unrealistic demands that they place on themselves and others. This is a cognitive distortion that is translated into "shoulds," "oughts," "have tos," and "musts," as well as the opposite "should not," "ought not," and "must not." Such ideas need to be challenged and reframed so that a more realistic and useful perspective can be adopted to move forward.

As you reflect on this point of finding a way to move forward, what ideas do you have about what you *should do* and about how you *ought to* move forward? Is it feasible at this time? If it is feasible, have you begun, or when will you begin? If it is not feasible, what other possible way exists? There is something else that you can do to move forward. It might mean reworking the idea or even coming up with an entirely new idea. In other words, if the original thought you had about what you would do to go forward is not working out, go back to the drawing board. You might not find the way in a moment, but keep brainstorming. You will figure it out.

As I write this section, I reflect on my own path to writing this book. I have long wanted to be involved in professional development but was stuck on doing so with educators. Much of my working life has been in the classroom, a large part of which was spent as a teacher educator. I have thus been desirous of working with teachers as I have observed areas that could be strengthened to facilitate more effective teaching and learning. My initial ideas were therefore geared towards developing training sessions and writing texts to be used in the education sector. I had the thought that I *ought to* do my significant work in the education sector and with educators because that is the field in which I had done most of my work and had much training.

I tried in various ways to get going with training and writing in the education sector but found it was not working. However, I would not explore other options for a while because I was stuck on finding a way to do what I desired to do with educators, because, in my mind, that was what I *should* do. It was not until I realized that while it would be nice to work with educators, there was nothing that said I *should, ought to,* or *must* do so first or only in that sector that I was able to explore other ideas that would help me to add value to people using words. I had to get past the shoulds, ought tos, and musts that were limiting me in order to move forward.

As was happening in my life, are you at a point where you are stuck, not able to progress in some area because what you have thought about doing or how you have envisioned things happening is just not working out? Is there any should, ought to, or must that you might need to reframe in your own life to move forward in that area?

I find the first part of the Rotary Club's four-way test to be useful in dealing with such cognitive distortions. One is advised to ask, "Is it the truth?" This requires thinking about your thinking. An examination of one's thoughts should lead to a change in thinking where it is recognized that those shoulds, ought tos, and musts are not true. A further encouragement on this wise is found in the Scriptures in Philippians 4:8, where one is admonished to focus on things that are true, among others. Indeed, according to John 8:32, knowledge of the truth sets one free. When you know the truth and walk in that truth, then you will engage in actions based on that truth that will lead to progress and advancement, thus moving forward.

As it pertains to taking action, it is not true that the first idea or idea that you have settled on is how things should, ought to, or must be done to be successful. I have found that the initial idea is often useful to get the ball rolling and start the process but might not be the ultimate solution. Usually, the idea that you have thought about or might have settled on can be refined and expanded through further thinking and discussions as others become involved in deliberating about the idea.

At a recent International Maxwell Conference, the leadership expert John Maxwell indicated in a presentation on personal growth that one way to grow is to share. He pointed out that thoughts can be expanded through shared thinking. He said, "Some of our best thinking will be done by others."

If this is so, it means that whatever thoughts or ideas you might have about a matter are limited. Something else can be added or another perspective can be seen when it is shared, and others get involved in thinking through the issue with you.

> *A thought or idea has not grown enough to be considered to be enough if it has not expanded through shared thinking. Bring others into your thinking space to go forward.*

This suggests that an idea not exposed to shared thinking remains limited. Therefore, to think that any idea you have about something is the way it should, ought to, or must happen would not be the truth. Until it is shared and expanded through collective thinking, it has not grown enough to be considered to be enough. Said another way, until you have invited others into your thinking on a matter, the idea or thought is limited and might not be the best or most effective. A thought or idea cannot be said to be complete if it has not expanded through shared thinking.

This brings into focus another issue: the extent to which you are open to and engage others in reflecting on the ideas and thoughts that you have. In my own case, I had mentioned the idea of going into professional development targeting educators to my husband, and we spoke about it. The conversation was centered around my idea of how I saw the business and how I was going to execute it and not a true discussion and thinking on the matter that resulted in an expansion of the idea.

In fact, when the idea was mentioned to another good friend who was also an entrepreneur, she suggested considering other target markets and tweaking my offering to reach out to other businesses and industries besides education. At the time, I did not seriously consider the suggestion and even resisted it in my mind as I was bent on reaching out first to educators. Others could be helped in the process, but education would be my field of operation, I thought. I insisted on this in my mind. I was not open to other thinking that would truly expand the idea.

And what do you know? I ran with my idea, but the business did not take off. I remained stuck with a desire to do something more to add value to others while having more flexibility, financial security, and general peace of mind. It was not until I truly invited others into my thinking and became open to other ideas and possibilities of how to effectively use what I have that I became unstuck and began to go forward. I had to let go of the shoulds, the ought tos, and the musts that were holding me back from doing what I was created to do.

Who have you spoken to about the thought or idea you have? There are friends, family members, associates, and partners who might be able to shed some additional light on the matter as they share new perspectives. Reach out to them and be open to hearing and considering the options they present.

You might not want to share your thoughts or ideas with people who are close to you based on the situation. The good news is that other options are available for you to share and get feedback that will expand your thoughts and help you to move forward. There are different types of professionals who can help. For example, talking to a counsellor might be a good idea if there are some problems or unresolved issues from your past that are associated with the thoughts that have kept you stuck. If, however, you are more concerned with exploring an idea or achieving some goal and need some support and guidance, then talking to a coach would be helpful.

Whatever your choice, it is important to bring others into your thinking space to help you move forward. Dealing with musterbation as you reframe shoulds, ought tos, and musts through shared thinking can be one strategy for moving from being stuck to experiencing greater abundance in various aspects of life.

Perspectives on Moving Forward

Taking Steps

A typical walk consists of a repeated gait cycle involving two phases: the stance and swing phases. The stance phase involves a heel strike as the foot hits the ground heel first. It also involves a support stage as the rest of the leading foot hits the ground, and the muscles work to cope with the force passing through the leg. The final stage in the stance phase is the toe-off phase as the leading foot prepares to leave the ground—heels first, toes last.

The swing phase of walking involves the leg lift when the lower limb is raised in preparation for the swing stage once the foot has left the ground. The final phase in the walking cycle is the swing phase, where the raised leg is propelled forward. This is where the forward motion of the walk occurs.[13]

The process of going forward by walking involves taking steps, whether aided or unaided. It requires bracing oneself from a sitting, lying, kneeling or other position, putting one leg in front of the other, and doing so, step by step, to go forward in the repeated gait cycle. People who are unable to move forward by walking usually use a wheelchair. The rider is propelled forward with every revolution of the wheel.

A step or a revolution represents one unit of movement. Going forward begins with just one unit of movement. It starts with one step or one rotation of the wheel.

John Maxwell has noted that "every big thing that's ever been done started with a first step." He adds, "We can't get anywhere in life without taking that first small step."[14]

It is important to do that one thing that will begin the process of going forward, and then keep doing so until you have advanced far enough. Take that first step and keep going. Get that wheel turning. The journey of a thousand miles does begin with one step. What is that one thing that you need to

---

[13] Teach Me Anatomy. (nd). *Walking and gaits*. Retrieved from https://teachmeanatomy.info/lower-limb/misc/walking-and-gaits/

[14] Maxwell, J. (2015). *Intentional living: Choosing a life that matters.* Center Street. (page 56).

do—the one step you need to take—to begin the process of going forward?

Is it finding one positive thing to focus on daily or identifying that thing you will affirm about yourself daily? Is it making that decision to read something educational or inspirational for at least thirty minutes every day? Yes, give up thirty minutes on social media. Is it taking the time to work on that talent that you have every

> *Begin where you are. What is in the distance will eventually come closer into view as you take steps or make revolutions toward it.*

day? Yes, carve out the time from the time spent playing those incessant games or watching those videos, movies, or series that you are hooked on.

In my country, Jamaica, there are some proverbs in the dialect that are useful in understanding the value of making the effort to do small or seemingly simple things that will eventually pay dividends. One idiom is, "Every mickle mek a muckle," which means that small things, when combined one by one, can have a big effect. Another saying is, "One, one coco full basket." English translation: one by one, each cocoa can fill a basket, or gathering one coco at a time will fill the basket. This means that the path to success is a step-by-step process. Success does not come suddenly.

James Clear's exposition on the power of tiny gains in his book *Atomic Habits* supports this point. He says, "Excellence is not about radical change but accruing small improvements over time."[15] He explains that what starts out small and may be relatively insignificant has consequences as it compounds over time. Therefore, "Getting 1% better every day counts for a lot in the long run."[16] The conclusion: doing small things or taking small steps in the direction you desire to go will matter in time.

Every minute spent working on that area of strength will eventually get you to the 10,000 hours that Malcolm Gladwell suggests is required to achieve mastery, as he explains in his book *Outliers*. It might mean going to sleep just half an hour later as you put in time every day to get the wheels turning on that thing you have wanted to achieve for so long. If you are like me, you would have gone to bed and would have taken a while to fall asleep anyway, as you would have been tossing and turning with thoughts of everything else on your mind. So why not use the time more productively until you are really ready to sleep?

It is important to see the value in making small steps and doing little things that matter. Too often, persons do not move forward as they are overly focused on what seems like a gargantuan task to be accomplished. This tends to happen when the focus is on being farther along the path than your present capabilities can deal with. This could mean having expectations associated with being at the end without taking

---

[15] James Clear. Keynote presentation at International Maxwell Conference August 14, 2023.

[16] Clear, J. (2018). *Atomic Habits*. Found in Chapter 1 Summary (Kindle Version). Penguin Random House

into consideration the realties of your current position and the fact that it takes time to move forward.

Yes, the command is to go forward; however, you are not expected to make a giant leap to reach 12,000 miles immediately. Instead of focusing on not being able to play the oboe like someone who has been practicing for years, think about the effort you can put into practicing every day to become like that master player in the time to come. Begin where you are. What is in the distance will eventually come closer into view as you take steps or make revolutions toward it.

This brings into focus the issue of perspective as you seek to go forward. What are you looking at as you go forward? While you need to have big dreams, you also need to be prepared to work with the immediate, seemingly simple realities to achieve those dreams. Some persons have unrealistic expectations and ideas. They want it all now.

We live in a fast-paced world where instant gratification is desired. I see it, and I want it now. Why wait? This approach will not work with moving forward unless the distance to be travelled is immediately in front of your nose. It takes time to travel some distance. There is no genie or magic wand that is going to make you instantaneously appear at the end of the road. Time and effort will be required to go forward to that destination. How much time and effort are you willing to invest daily, weekly, and monthly to move forward? Yes, what are those steps—small or big—that you will take to move forward?

Persistence and Consistency

Notice the word *steps*. It is plural. It means more than one. It means persistence in continuing to take one step after another until the journey is completed, the destination has been reached, and the objective or goal has been achieved. Going forward requires that you continue to take steps.

One step will not get you to the destination. It is good to begin. It is good to take the first step; however, one step is not good enough. Taking one step and stopping will not project you much further than where you were. You need to do things that take you out of sight of where you originally began to effectively go forward. While you might not forget your starting point or places along the journey, if what is within your view or eyesight is still the outline of where you are coming from, it might mean that you have not travelled far enough. You have not taken enough steps.

This brings to mind my experience of travelling to other countries. When the airplane takes off, as I look out the window, I can make out familiar buildings and streets. I usually try to see if I can identify places that I know or know about as I relish the experience. Distinct buildings and places give way to outlines and then landforms that are too distant to be specifically identified. You eventually get to a point where the airplane has gone so high and so far that the city or country where the flight began is no longer in sight. The landmass or body of water above which the airplane flies is a different territory. You always get to a point where the place you have left is only a memory that is no longer visible.

Continuous motion is necessary to go to a different territory, a new place, another place where there will be new encounters and enriching experiences. Continuous motion requires persistence and consistency. You always have to be cognizant of the destination.

Persistence will require repeating your efforts, doing it over and over, again and again—taking one step after another. It means not getting tired of doing the right thing—not getting tired of doing the same thing. It also means pushing beyond obstacles to do what needs to be done repeatedly.

Repeatedly doing the same thing over time builds a habit. Certainly, habits lead to outcomes. Positive outcomes require positive habits. Developing positive habits in line with desired outcomes is necessary as part of the steps to go forward in an area. James Clear has outlined four laws or stages in the process of habit formation in his book *Atomic Habits*. Utilizing those laws or any other system that will help one to be persistent in taking the necessary steps to move forward is worth doing.

In the Scriptures, readers are encouraged in Galatians 6:9 not to grow weary in doing what is right because one will reap the rewards in due season if one does not give up. Indeed, going forward will require making a commitment to keep doing what is necessary for as long as it takes, despite the obstacles, until the destination is reached.

A plane that stops midflight spells disaster. Do not let your journey end in disaster. Make that commitment. Keep going.

Get Information

You might find that the steps are easier than you thought when you have accurate information about what you need to do. It is important to seek out information about what you desire to do to help make decisions about moving forward. Information will help to give perspective as you better understand what is involved in the process and, therefore, can be more realistic in planning and approaching the task. Some persons have been paralyzed by what they consider a mammoth task—the giant step—and, as a result, have not moved forward.

Every task can usually be broken down into steps and sub-steps. Aim to complete the task step by step. Even as you keep the bigger picture in view, focus on each step to be completed. This can be accomplished as you seek to understand the task to be done and use that understanding to set goals, objectives, and timelines and decide on resources that will be required. Take small steps if you need to until you can take larger ones. Get information to help determine the steps you need to take.

Information can be acquired through your own research. Books, videos, documents, artifacts, and creative works can be sources of information. These represent both primary and secondary sources of information. Communication with persons with knowledge and experience in the area where you desire to move forward is also a good way to acquire information. Chandler Bolt suggests that in order to get help, you should ask who, not how—finding the right people who will introduce you to the how.[17]

It is important to take time to learn about the area in which you desire to move forward. This is one action that could be considered a necessary condition to move forward effectively. With information, you can count the cost and put things in place to keep the momentum. Without information, the task of moving forward could become more daunting. This could lead to paralysis, with you being unable to move, or you might stumble along as you try to figure out what needs to be done.

I have found this to be true in my own life. I had many questions about what I needed to do to become a published author. It was hard to move forward for a while as I was unsure what I was doing. The high C in me made the task even more daunting as I needed to have details. I need to have specific details. I had an idea, but how to turn it into a book, and not just any book, eluded me for a while. I desired to write and publish a book of high quality that hundreds and eventually millions of people would read. It would not be good enough to have a book published to say I have written a book. It needed to have an impact, and I needed the know-how to do that.

Yes, I had written academic papers and even had a few publications in journals, but writing a book was not the same. I had begun to do some writing, making use of some of the principles and skills I had acquired from writing in academia and preparing for sermons and presentations. It, however, was

---

[17] Chandler Bolt webinar on publishing

not working. I felt stuck and unsure of what I was doing for some time. Persons kept asking, "When are you going to write a book?" This was partly why it was not forthcoming. I needed more information to make the dream of putting inspired life-transforming words into the hands of people a reality.

Recognizing the lack of information as a limitation in my quest to become a best-selling author, I set about to find help. Chandler Bolt's book *Published* was a very good starting point in helping me to unpack the writing process. I also got more individualized help by making the financial investment to participate in a coaching programme for authors facilitated by DayeLight Publishers. When Coach Crystal helped me to work through my message and helped shape the title and chapters for the book, I knew I had found the light. No doubt you can attest to this as you are now reading this book.

What do you desire to know that would help you move forward more effectively? What is it that is challenging you as you seek to move forward that you might need to learn more about? In what way might you need to grow to be able to go forward? What format(s) will you use to get the necessary information, and when will you begin? Who do you need to talk to or get information from, and how can you meet the person? Your responses to these questions present opportunities for expanding your knowledge in the area in which you desire to go and grow.

Make a promise to yourself to do what you need to do to get the necessary information to move forward. Fulfil that promise to yourself.

Accepting Your Reality

Another perspective in going forward is accepting your reality. The prayer of serenity attributed to Reinhold Niebuhr is very apt. It says, "Father, give us courage to change what must be altered, serenity to accept what cannot be helped, and the insight to know the one from the other."[18] Accepting your reality includes accepting the circumstances surrounding your life and the situations about yourself that impact your movement. There are some things about our lives and circumstances that we cannot change. In his book *No Limits: Blow the Cap off Your Capacity*, John Maxwell refers to these as birth caps and life caps.

Kevin had a birth cap. He had no control over the condition that he was born with, nor could he go back in time and change it. He has had to and will have to continue to live with the effects of Arthrogryposis. Life caps represent things that happen in life that you cannot control. We lose people and things that we love. We experience accidents and illnesses.

It is important to accept the birth and life caps that we cannot change to go forward. It does not mean that you have to like or even love it, but you need to accept it and deal with it to move forward. With such an acceptance, you can direct energy towards addressing issues over

> *Stop wasting energy worrying over things you cannot change. Spend that time investing in areas of potential that will make a difference.*

---

[18] Retrieved from https://www.catholic.com/qa/did-st-francis-really-create-the-serenity-prayer

which you have control in life, which can propel you forward. Wasting time and energy bemoaning things that you cannot change will keep you stuck in a place of regret and unhappiness instead of moving forward to a place of joy, peace, and happiness.

Yes, Kevin's reality was that he was born with a condition that made him unable to walk unaided for the rest of his life. I definitely do not think he would ever say, "I love having Arthrogryposis." He however needed to accept that reality to go forward the way he has been able to.

Not having things perfect doesn't mean you cannot go forward. That is where some people are challenged. They are waiting for things to be perfect to move forward. To take such a position, you might never move forward as it is hard to find anything that is perfect in this life. You need to accept where you are and the circumstances related to your movement and take the necessary action based on that. Yes, take that step or get the wheels turning.

Kevin wanted to learn to swim. He believed that it was possible despite being differently abled. He knew his limitations and sought the necessary help. He has been getting support from others, like his swimming instructor. Despite the limitations, he is going forward.

Accepting the reality of those with whom we have to associate in moving forward is also important. For example, while you would like it another way, you cannot change your child's personality or mental capacity, so you need to accept her for how she is and deal with it. You might, for example, have a child with slow processing speed and a neurological disorder that affects academic performance and general living. That is your reality. Or, you might have a child on the autism spectrum. That is your reality. Whatever the medical, physical, or psychological situation with your child, it is your reality.

Having faith in God and His ability to heal won't make your child's situation go away if God does not choose to heal. One can pray to God, but one cannot determine how He responds or deals with the situation. God is sovereign, and so can choose to act how He pleases just as man has free will. We must deal with the realities of our humanity and world, be it related to our children or any other person in our lives. We also have to live with the consequences of choices, both of ours and others. Many of these are things we cannot change.

Accepting things that we cannot change and directing energy towards doing other things that will actually make a positive difference in the situation are important steps in going forward. Is there any situation in your life that you cannot seem to move past and that you wish was different? Take a moment to analyze the situation. Is it something that you can change? If it is something you cannot change, please accept that it is what it is and there is nothing you can do to change it. You might need to say this to yourself a few or many times: *"It is what it is. There is nothing that I can do to change it, so I will stop worrying about it."*

Now, direct your attention to the things that you can do to deal with it and make the most of what you have. You can grow. You can experience a positive increase. Things can get better in spite of the birth or life caps. There is potential in every situation. Set your focus on finding that area of potential and investing in it.

Stop wasting energy worrying over things you cannot change. Spend that time investing in areas of potential that will make a difference. Spend your time doing things that matter. Do things that will positively affect the people and the situation you are dealing with. Do things that will help you maximize the potential that exists despite the situation.

Dealing with Feelings

Your feelings are also a part of your reality that need to be accepted and dealt with to move forward. Your feelings give an indication of what is going on with you. Don't deny them; pay attention to them. Your feelings are telling you something; listen!

Find out what is leading to the feelings you are experiencing and deal with it accordingly. Keep doing the things that are leading to positive feelings and make adjustments in areas that are leading to negative feelings. The more positive you are, the greater energy you will have to move forward.

While you should do everything in your power to have positive emotions, this will not always be so. There are days when you will not feel very positive. Going forward, however, does not mean that you are always going to feel good; you keep going anyway. Keep doing the right thing regardless of how you feel. Keep doing the right thing even when you don't like it, and you don't understand. This admonition is echoed in the Scriptures in Galatians 6:9, where readers are encouraged not to get tired of doing the right thing because they will be rewarded at the right time.

Don't make *liking* a criterion for doing things that you need to do to move forward. You might not like it and might even feel afraid, but you need to do it once it is the right thing to do. My mentor, Valorie Burton, says, "One can still feel fear and move forward, so don't let fear make a decision for you." It is okay to hug the monster. Do it afraid.

Moving forward is partly about understanding what needs to be done and doing the right thing in the moment. There are many things that are useful but not pleasant. Getting an injection to prevent or treat some illnesses might not be pleasant, and it is certainly not a procedure that many like. However, not taking a necessary inoculation because you do not like it could lead to many issues that could jeopardize forward movement in numerous ways.

> *Don't make liking a criterion for doing things that you need to do to move forward. Don't let the things you don't like keep you from experiencing the things you do like when you move forward.*

What do you need to do to move forward that you do not like to do? Muster up the courage and do it anyway. Don't give things you don't like power over you. Don't allow the things you don't like to control you. To do so will cause the things you don't like to keep you from experiencing the things you do like when you move forward. Giving in to what you don't like could keep you from going forward.

81

Pace

One might ask, "How fast should I move?" or "How slowly?" My response would be to go as fast as you are able to. Go as far as is possible, as fast as you can, as you run your own race. Some people are on a 100-metre dash. Others are running a 5000-metre-long distance race. There are others doing a marathon. Your race will determine your pace. Understanding the race you are in is important.

Although contemporaries, David Rudisha, the 800-metre champion from Kenya, dare not run like Usain Bolt, the 100 and 200 metres champion from Jamaica. It requires different strategies and pace to be able to hold out for 1 minute 40:91 seconds on the 800-metre track as against 19:19 seconds in a 100-metre sprint. Usain Bolt had better get up quickly and accelerate fast down that track. He has only a short distance to go. David Rudisha, on the other hand, after getting out of the blocks fast as well, will need to bide his time maintaining certain speeds as he travels specific distances, gradually accelerating until he gets to the end. Pacing is critical for endurance in the longer race. Accelerating fast and trying to maintain a fast pace throughout the longer race would not do David well if he wanted to endure to the end of his race and be very successful.

The importance of pace in relation to the race being run was brilliantly brought out in the 2016 film *Remember the Goal* and the 2019 spin-off *The Perfect Race*. Coach Courtney Smith-Donnelly worked with a girl's cross-country team to lead them to their first ever state title and a female athlete to achieve success in an 800-metre run. Interestingly, as the coach sought to implement strategies to develop the athletes in preparing them for the competitions, pace was a similar concern in both movies. Parents, other coaches, and even some of the athletes thought Coach Smith-Donnelly had the girls running too slowly and were very distraught that they were going to lose. However, the coach's insistence on the athletes remembering and understanding the goal caught my attention.

For the girls' cross-country team, while the ultimate goal was winning the state championship, there were other goals for each meet leading up to the finals. It was important that the team was prepared enough and engaged in the specific strategy to meet the goal for each race. Onlookers were always concerned about being first or as close as possible to first in each race or competition and so were upset when Donnelly's team barely made it. Coach Donnelly was always clear that the goal was winning the state title. Therefore, not winning the other competitions was not a big deal once the team successfully made it to the next round.

For Coach Donnelly, each race was part of preparing for the final competition, which really mattered. She did not want to have the team running too fast too quickly when it was not necessary but have them gain enough strength and stamina to speed up when they needed to in the race that mattered. While many were concerned about what other teams were doing or how strong other teams were, the coach looked at her athletes' strengths and weaknesses and built them individually to do their best to contribute to the overall team's success. The coach had each girl run her own race at her own pace within the team, bearing in mind the specific requirements for each competition. It worked. They qualified for each successive competition until they got to the finals, where they became the champions.

How often do we get distracted by what others are doing that we try to go as fast as they are going and find that we cannot keep pace? We compare ourselves with them, not realizing that our circumstances are not the same. To match what we think they have, we try to do exactly what they are doing, believing that it will make us just like them or better. How often are we swayed by the suggestions of onlookers who do not work directly with us in the trenches but often offer unsolicited advice from their 20/70 perspective? How often do we overlook the smaller goals related to the present circumstance that cause us to put ourselves and others under undue stress to take unnecessary action, wanting them to go at a pace that is faster than required for the immediate goal?

Yes, you need to go forward. Indeed, it is imperative that you go forward. You, however, need to do so at a comfortable pace, while ensuring that you are maximizing your potential. Yes, you need to take that step, but do you walk slowly, briskly, jog, sprint, or run at a moderate pace? Do you push the wheelchair fast or slow down the path?

A number of factors are to be borne in mind when deciding on the pace at which you should move forward. Firstly, the distance to be travelled must be considered. How long will you need to be doing this thing for? For an activity that needs to be sustained over a long period, it is useful to have it broken down into manageable portions that you will be likely to engage in consistently until the task is done. How much of each day or week can you dedicate to the activity to get it done? How often will you do it, and for how long? How much will you do at each sitting? When do you hope to complete it? These are some questions to be answered as you prepare to continue to take steps to move forward for the long haul.

Another factor to consider is your fitness level and general condition and health to be able to undertake the task. How much can you do, and for how long? As human beings, it is important to be realistic about our humanity. We have a physical capacity to do some things and not others. Similarly, we have emotional and cognitive capacities. We should recognize what we are able to do and other things that will be a challenge. This understanding should guide how much we take on and for how long. We should learn to be true to ourselves. Others might have done it in two weeks with their circumstances. You might need a month to get it done, and that is okay. This is a part of accepting your reality. Pace yourself to get the task done based on what you can realistically manage.

A final consideration in setting the pace is the requirements for the task to be completed to move you forward. Is it timebound? Are there specific conditions to be met within a certain timeframe? How flexible is the timeframe? Is it internally or externally imposed? How fast will you need to work to meet the conditions? Answers to these questions will also be useful in helping you set the pace for how you will work to move forward. Working towards objectives and goals is crucial in going forward, but it needs to be done at a reasonable pace.

It certainly would have been nice to get this book done between three and six months as I was encouraged to do. Who would not want an earlier publication? I found, however, that with all my other responsibilities and the circumstances of my life, working at a pace that would facilitate publication within the short window would have placed me under significant strain. I had to work slower for my overall health and well-being and to be adequately able to function in other areas of life. I had to choose a slower pace. Find your pace. Work with the pace that is right for you. Go forward!

Reflections and Notes

How have your perspectives been transformed based on the concepts that were highlighted in this chapter? How will you respond to the issues raised in this chapter as you go forward?

_____

_____

_____

_____

_____

_____

_____

_____

_____

_____

_____

_____

_____

_____

_____

_____

_____

_____

_____

_____

_____

_____

_____

_____

_____

_____

_____

_____

_____

_____

_____

_____

_____

CHAPTER 4

HOW FAR FORWARD SHOULD I GO?

On a trip from the Norman Manley International Airport in Kingston, Jamaica, to the Lester B. Pearson International Airport in Ontario, Canada, you would expect to travel approximately 1786 miles or 2876 kilometres. With the navigation features available via the in-flight app, you are able to determine how much of the distance has been covered and how far away you are from the destination.

On the other hand, I can imagine the countless times children and adult passengers alike would ask, "Are we there yet?" when the destination is not known. This question from travelers usually means, have we just about arrived at the expected destination, or are we in the vicinity?

These scenarios and other experiences highlight some important considerations with respect to distance as you move forward. It is relatively easy to determine distance when the exact destination is known. There is also an inherent desire to know where you are going and where you are in relation to

---

where you are going. What, however, do you do when the exact distance is not known or there are challenges in going the distance?

Going the Distance

There are times in going forward when you know where you are to go. If your desire is to become a teacher of science, then it is clear that acquiring certification as a teacher will be necessary. Yet, getting any teacher's certificate will not do. If the aim is to teach science, then specializing in English, Social Studies, or some other subject that is not science-based will not be sufficient. Until you have attained certification to teach science at the desired level of the education system, the destination for that leg of the journey has not been reached. It would be prudent to keep going until it is attained.

You should be careful not to mistake stops along the journey for the destination or otherwise turn a stop along the journey into the destination. For example, if the opportunity arises to serve as a substitute or assistant teacher, it would be useful to function in the role if feasible. The experience to be gained could be invaluable in the future. No experience is wasted. Too often, however, some persons settle for remaining a substitute or assistant teacher in general courses when the original goal of becoming a science teacher remains unfulfilled. You have not gone the distance or far enough if the intended destination has not been reached. No matter how close it is to the destination, close is not far enough.

An experience I had as an undergraduate student has helped to underscore this point in my own life. I was a member of the University and Colleges Apostolic Ministries (UCAM) while I was completing my first degree. In keeping with its motto: *unity, fellowship, and evangelism*, the group frequently planned activities that engaged participants spiritually and socially. One such activity was a hike to the lovely Blue Mountain Peak, the highest point in Jamaica. The peak forms part of the Blue and John Crow Mountain National Park, which was named a UNESCO World Heritage Site in 2015.

I eagerly prepared for the trip, maintaining my fitness level to avoid possible illness and injury before and on the hike. I got myself the essentials for the hike, including comfortable sneakers, rain gear, and warm clothing. I packed just enough snacks and

> *Be careful not to mistake stops along the journey for the destination or otherwise turn a stop along the journey into the destination.*

liquid refreshments in a knapsack that I could reasonably carry as I scaled the mountain heights.

I set off with the group on a Friday night to be at the Blue Mountain Peak by dawn on Saturday morning. We travelled via motor vehicle from Papine to Mavis Bank, where the hike began. With steely determination and the spirit of unity, the group forged ahead on foot up the narrow, rugged, and steep path. Listening keenly to the able guide, and with encouraging words, songs, and a helping hand here and there, we conquered each hurdle one step at a time. In the cold and dark night, we made it past a number of landmarks, among which was the treacherous Jacob's Ladder, considered the steepest and worst portion of the trail. We eventually arrived at

Portland Gap, where we would rest for a few hours before climbing to the peak at sunrise.

I awoke later that morning, ready to complete the climb. I anticipated the hustle and bustle as my fellow hikers and I gathered our belongings to continue our journey up the mountain. Our tour guide would give further instructions that would see us arriving at the peak in about three hours or so, in time to see the majesty of the mountains at sunrise.

Things were, however, not moving as fast as I had thought. I was not getting any communication. I was not hearing the directive to be up and about to get going. I started to wonder what was happening; how long would it be before we continued the climb?

My inquiry revealed that the group would no longer be making the trek to the peak. Where we were at Portland Gap would be the final destination. The decision had been taken on behalf of the majority of the team that we would not continue the climb. Ironically, although we had completed the hardest part of the climb earlier in the night, it was felt that whatever had happened during the few hours we had stopped made continuing on not a good idea. Apparently, rain fell during the night, and the organizers believed that it was now dangerous to continue the climb.

Had the situation occurred today, I would have found a way to make it to the top. However, as a freshman with very little exposure to the ways of the world, limited resources, and unsure of myself, while my heart sank on the inside, I could not put up much of a fight. There were real dangers associated with the climb that I could not handle without others. Trying to do so on my own would have been foolhardy. While I asked and earnestly desired to continue towards the goal, I was outnumbered by those who were satisfied with the attempt but did not want to go the distance. That was one time when a stop along the journey became the destination. I had not gone far enough.

After over twenty years, I still look back with regret. Reaching the Blue Mountain Peak is something I have yet to accomplish. I look forward to repeating the experience, this time making it to the peak. The spiritual and life lessons learned from the experience of the climb have not been able to compensate for the loss of whatever else would have been experienced at the top of the peak. Portland Gap at 1795 metres was not far enough. The destination was the Blue Mountain Peak, 461 metres higher, which was not achieved. I had not gone forward far enough.

How often have you found yourself in such a situation? A place that should have been a temporary stop has become a place of permanent residence. Something that should have been a temporary solution has become a permanent fixture. Something that should have ended some time ago is being continued indefinitely. In what way is this true in some aspect of your life—relationship, career, education, health, finances, spirituality?

What are your goals and dreams? Are you on the way to achieving them? Are you moving forward, or have you stopped with no specific timeline to move toward the next milestone? If you are on your way to achieving your goal, keep going forward. There is yet some distance to be covered. Keep pressing toward your *Destination—Goal* or *Destination—Dream.*

If, on the other hand, you have stopped, it is time to take stock of where you are. What is happening at the place where you are? Are you willing to settle for where you are instead of your original goal or dream? What are you holding on to at the place where you are that you should have let go of or have given up a while ago that is hindering your forward movement?

Indeed, you might have come a long way from where you

> *If where you are is not the best place that you could possibly be given all the circumstances, then where you are is not far enough.*

began. However, if where you are is not the best place that you could possibly be, all things being considered, then where you are is not far enough. While every effort to move forward must be commended, I would not mean you well if I did not help you to recognize that going forward for you will mean going farther. Don't settle for less than the best that is possible, given your circumstances.

Yes, approximately 11.1 miles (17.9 km) was a far distance to have walked up the mountain and a significant feat, especially given the terrain. However, that 3.5 miles (5.6 km) from Portland Gap was an additional distance that should have been travelled to reach the destination at the peak. Portland Gap was not far enough.

If that goal is still attainable and viable, you have not gone far enough until the goal has been achieved and the dream fulfilled. Distance is not just measured by miles but also by the amount of ground covered to get to the desired destination.

What or where is your Portland Gap? What is the "gap" between where you are and where you should be going? Find a way to close that gap as you go forward. Until that gap is closed, you have not gone far enough. Challenge yourself to go the distance. Challenge yourself to persevere and be persistent in pursuit of your passion. Practice grit.[19]

When the Distance is Longer Than Expected

While the distance from Kingston, Jamaica to Toronto, Ontario by airplane is approximately 1786 miles or 2876 kilometres, that is not the entire distance that must be travelled. Everyone on that Air Canada flight has travelled and will travel a different distance.

You see, while the starting point for the flight was from the airport, the journey would have begun before the flight and would continue after the flight ended unless the ultimate destination was the airport. Passengers travel from various locations across the parishes to the Norman Manley International Airport. After arriving at the Canadian airport, passengers will also travel different distances to arrive at their respective destinations. This means that people travel different distances to get from Jamaica to Canada.

Each traveler's circumstance will determine how far he or she will need to travel to get to the destination. Preparation

---

[19] See Angela Duckworth's writing on the subject in Grit: The Power of Passion and Perseverance

will need to be made by travelers to travel the distance for the various segments of the trip. It is important to know where you are in relation to where you want to go; the starting and end points. The difference between these points will determine the distance to be travelled and the way one travels.

The journey to the vacation is not just from Jamaica to Canada but from a specific address in Jamaica to a specific address in Canada. Getting from Mona in Kingston, Jamaica, to Brampton, Ontario in Canada, is a shorter distance and will require different arrangements than the trip from Hill Sixty, Trelawny, to Wyandotte Street, Windsor, in the respective countries. The specifics matter.

Where are you travelling from? What are the circumstances associated with where you are and where you are going? Understanding the specific circumstances surrounding your life is crucial in determining how far you will need to travel and how long it might take to move forward. These should be borne in mind, and you should plan accordingly.

Let us look at two students born in the same year and who desire to maximize their potential by obtaining a degree in an area of interest. Abigail and Katherine were two lovely girls who met in preparatory school. They were equally smart, disciplined, and very involved in school life, albeit they had different interests. They both did very well in the primary exit examination and were accepted into the same prestigious high school. They did not wane in their positive attitude and diligence to work, and so continued to excel.

As they progressed, it became apparent that it was getting harder and harder for Katherine to keep up. It took her longer to complete tasks, and inordinate effort was required to continue performing at the level at which she had been operating. Katherine was eventually diagnosed with a neurodevelopmental disorder and slow processing. This would change the trajectory of her life.

Both girls continued to aspire to excel and accomplish great things as they worked to the best of their ability. However, as one might imagine, it became increasingly harder for Katherine to achieve her dreams. Abigail progressed normally through the school system, completing coursework, taking, and passing examinations with the highest honours at every level, being highly involved in various extra-curricular activities and leadership, and more or less sailing through. This was not so for Katherine.

Katherine attended four different secondary level/pre-university institutions as attempts were made to give her the support needed to deal with the various challenges that were unearthed. She had to give up many things along the way as her brain processing capacity would not allow her to be able to do more than one thing at a time. Fortunately, she eventually made it to university through a circuitous and arduous route. Her time at university to complete her degree was also longer. Katherine could not carry a regular load and struggled greatly to manage the courses. It would take all her willpower and much support from family and healthcare practitioners to complete the degree.

Abigail and Katherine had similar aspirations and were both conscientious and diligent in their attitude and approach to their studies. They were on a similar journey but travelled different routes and distances to get to their respective destinations. They started in the same general area and went in a similar direction, but their circumstances differed. The distance travelled was tied to each person's circumstance.

Without any roadblocks, Abigail could proceed along the standard path, taking the regular route to her destination. Katherine had encountered major roadblocks and had to divert to other routes, which made the journey longer, eventually getting her to her destination. Importantly, both girls kept moving forward toward the destination. It was easier for Abigail than it had been for Katherine, but both girls kept going forward. Katherine had to come to grips with the reality of her challenges and travel the path that could accommodate her.

It is true that both girls initially would have had similar projections about the path and distance that would need to be travelled to get to their *destination (degree)*. However, life happened. She happened upon a life cap. The circumstances Katherine encountered significantly altered the path and distance she had to travel. How would you have dealt with the situation if you were Katherine? Would you have travelled the distance to get to the destination, or would you have given up?

Like each girl, we must live with our particular circumstances. We will need to make projections to go forward and alter them based on our reality. You should avoid the temptation to compare yourself with others, expecting your journey to be the same

> *Be prepared to take the journey travelling the distance that matches your reality.*

as others. The distance to be travelled might not be exactly the same if you do not have a similar reality. How far forward should you go then? It will depend on your reality. Be prepared to take the journey travelling the distance that matches your reality.

What do you do when the distance you intended to travel turns out to be longer than expected? Evaluate, recalculate, recalibrate, and keep going forward until you have arrived at the destination. Indeed, you should make plans about the path to take and the journey to be undertaken with the information at hand. You must, however, be willing to make adjustments if challenges are encountered along the way that create roadblocks that affect your movement. Be prepared to divert to another road that might take longer but will get you to the destination.

If you find yourself on a path going a longer distance than you had intended to travel, don't panic. Instead, rejoice in the fact that you are going forward. Also, take some time to evaluate where you are in relation to where you desire to go. If an alternate, shorter, reliable route is available to keep you going forward and get you to the required destination, exit at the safest place and take it.

You should maximize the use of opportunities and resources by making the best choices available. Always do the best you can with what you have. If you are not doing this, then you are wasting opportunities and resources. Don't travel a longer distance than you need to get to where you are going. Make a decision not to waste anything else in your life.

If the seemingly long path you are on is the best possible route, accept it for what it is. Stay on the route. Go the distance. Don't take shortcuts. You risk losing out when you take shortcuts. There are necessary skills, opportunities, and knowledge to be acquired on the best possible route that you will miss out on when you take a shortcut. Those things that one would have missed are generally critical for reaching the goal in the best way possible. Don't shortchange yourself by taking a shortcut. Love yourself enough to give yourself the best by going the distance. You cannot expect others to give you their best if you are not willing to first give yourself the best.

Don't let the length of the route deter you from going forward to the destination. There are too many persons who have never gone beyond a limited radius because that other place is "too far" and "it is going to take too long."

How far is too far or too long when you consider the rewards and/or benefits to be derived from reaching the destination? Would you rather remain in a place of depression and dejection, a fairly helpless and hopeless state, being primarily dependent on others when, through some effort, you could achieve something that increases your well-being, gives independence, and overall peace of mind? Your well-being and peace of mind are worth travelling that extra distance.

Whether or not you choose to travel the distance, remember that you are dwelling somewhere at all times. Where you choose to dwell will determine the state of your life, and you determine where you dwell. If you are dwelling in a place where your life is less than optimal, the sacrifice to travel that extra distance to get to a better place of health and wellbeing would be worth the time and effort. You cannot blame others for where you dwell. Circumstances might place you where you are, but you do not have to stay where you are. You can choose to go forward.

When the Location and Distance are not Known

In my country, there are some inland and deep rural areas that cannot be located via the global positioning system (GPS). One, therefore, has to rely on human guides for directions as the terrain is navigated to arrive at the destination. A typical conversation and journey with local guides could be like the following.

Traveler: "Good day, I am looking for the place UpTop Mountain. Do you know where that is?"

Local Guide 1: "Yes, yes, I know where that is. It's just up the road. It's not far. Just travel straight a few miles and you will reach soon.

Traveler says, "thank you" and continues on the way, not knowing how far *just up the road* or *a few miles* is or what *straight* really means. After travelling a good distance, a few minutes well, around many curves and corners, with no street signs, no other people on the road, he still has no clue where he is or how much further he has to go. He stops to ask directions from the next person he sees. He receives the following instructions.

Local Guide 2: "Travel straight until you come to a big East Indian mango tree. You can't miss it. When you come to a deep corner after that, it's not far from there."

Traveler continues on and thinks to himself, "That word *straight* again. How do I differentiate a mango tree from the many other trees along the road, and more specifically, an East Indian mango tree? How far is *'not far from there?'*"

After driving for many more miles, lots of curves and turns, off roads, missing turns, inquiring from other locals, and over an hour, the driver eventually reaches the place that was just up the road, not far, and around a corner.

Just how far did that driver in the deep rural area travel to get to UpTop Mountain? One might never be sure unless a note was being made of the odometer's reading at specific locations.

What do you do when you are unsure about the distance you must travel or how long it will take to get to the destination? My recommendation is that you should seek information and guidance from reputable sources who have some knowledge about the place or general area you desire to reach. Move forward based on the general directions given, aided by common sense and other related information that is already known.

My mentor, John Maxwell, says, "When you do what you know, you discover what you don't know, but if you wait until you know, you will not discover what you don't know. Life begins to be revealed to you when you take the journey." In this mentorship session, John was saying that it is important to take action before you have all the answers.

Don't fail to start the journey because you do not have all the specific details about the distance to the destination. The person who cannot move forward until everything or most things about the destination are known might find him or herself stuck in one place for a good while.

There are some things in life that should be adventurous. Going forward to that place can be one such adventure. Fill up the gas tank and have some spare cash for any eventuality. Get the car started and head in the general direction given.

> *When you do what you know, you discover what you don't know, but if you wait until you know, you will not discover what you don't know. Life begins to be revealed to you when you take the journey.*
> —John C. Maxwell

When was the last time you had an adventure? Some people's lives are very routine and devoid of adventure. Are you such a person?

As you are on your way, continue in the general direction given until you receive further instructions. Ask more questions along the way. Seek to get clarity where you don't understand, but keep moving forward.

As you move forward, you might find it useful to highlight and note landmarks to mark the distance travelled. My husband uses this activity to help him countdown to his destination. He celebrates the distance covered as he passes every parish border. This gives a sense of accomplishment and makes the lengthy journey less daunting. His immediate focus is not on the end of the journey but on reaching each milestone until he has arrived at the destination.

> *Don't be so focused on how far you have to go that you fail to acknowledge how far you have come.*

How far have you come from where you started? Take time to acknowledge and celebrate that at intervals. Don't be so focused on how far you have left to go that you fail to recognize and acknowledge how far you have come. This acknowledgment will give you the impetus to go even further.

Instead of focusing on how much farther you have to go, find markers and landmarks to celebrate along the way. Steve Gilliland would say, "Enjoy the ride." Make the best of the journey as you travel toward your destination; then, how far you have to travel won't matter as much.

Changing Direction

I am not sure about you, but I do not remember being on a journey where there was only one straight road. There are always roads leading off, a roundabout or some other junction. There is usually a turn somewhere on that journey.

Similarly, on the journey of life, there are intersections. These are points in time when decisions need to be made about the next action. Sometimes, you can continue straight ahead. At other times, you might need to turn right or left but still move forward. Knowing when to change direction is important. Otherwise, you could continue on a path that leads to a place that is not the desired or intended destination.

Every road leads somewhere, but there are some roads that you should not be on because anywhere and everywhere is not where you should be. Where a road leads to may not be where you ought to be going. You should not be on that road. Get off. Find a way to get onto and travel on a road that leads to where you are going.

There are a number of challenges with continuing on a road where you should not be. Firstly, if you are on the wrong road, you will not get to where you need to go. If you are not going where you should be going, it means that some purpose will not be fulfilled—something that you were supposed to do will not get done. Something that you were created to be will not be accomplished. You could be going forward but not in the right direction.

I have seen this happen in situations where people are not working in their area of strength or not doing things that they are passionate about—doing things that have their head but not their heart. I have previously shared a situation from my own journey that fits this scenario. I was doing well in getting an education, successfully moving from one level to another. Yes, I was going forward but was heading in the wrong direction.

It was important to be on the path that I was on at the primary level. The majority of my experiences at that level served as the foundation for what I would pursue in later life. Literacy, numeracy, and other basic competencies learned at the elementary level are necessary building blocks for everything else to be done in life. The move from primary school to high school was also an important part of my journey in acquiring the academic background to go forward to achieve my potential. At the primary school–high school intersection, I continued straight ahead.

I arrived at another intersection at the end of high school. While alternate paths were available, I was to travel straight ahead to sixth form to pursue GCE'A level subjects in the sciences. This was necessary since medicine was supposed to be my destination. However, while travelling the path towards medicine, it grew darker and darker. The walls were caving in, and I was imploding. I had continued straight ahead to pursue a degree in Zoology and Chemistry at the intersection of high school and post-secondary level pursuits. The journey was, however, becoming unbearable. I was not enjoying the ride, nor was I looking forward to arriving at the destination where I was heading. I needed to take the nearest exit, get into another vehicle, and head for another destination. Continuing straight ahead was not the best path for me. I needed to change direction.

> *Every road leads somewhere, but there are some roads that you should not be on because anywhere and everywhere is not where you should be.*

As in my case, travelling along the wrong path can lead to frustration and result in loss of time and resources. The road to get to the destination in psychology and counselling was longer than if I had been on a path toward that discipline from high school. A year was added to my undergraduate studies, and I had to take additional courses before pursuing my master's degree.

Where are you on your journey? Are you headed in the right direction? There is too much to do and accomplish in the limited lifetime we are allotted to waste time on a path that is not leading to fulfilment or accomplishing purpose. There is too much to be doing to be on a journey just for the fun of it. And, often, it is not a joyride. If you are not on the right path, change direction.

Unlike me, you might have set out with the intention to arrive at a desired location. If you are on the wrong road, no good intention can get you to the intended destination. You need to stop and check to see where you are in relation to the intended destination, reroute, and find your way to the path that takes you to where you should be going. An experience I had on a family trip illustrates this point well.

My family travelled from Canada to Boston, Massachusetts, one summer. We would be staying with some friends who live on Grove Street. We entered the street number and street name into the GPS and set off on the 8-hour drive. It was a lovely adventure with a few planned and unplanned stops on the way. We arrived in Boston and contacted our friends, letting them know we were just a few minutes away. We soon arrived at the location to which the GPS directed us, but there was a challenge. That was not the home of our friends.

Our intended destination was not where we had arrived at. We had traveled for hours, only to end up at the wrong place. Fortunately, we figured out the error. Grove Street in Beacon Hill and Grove Street in Randolph are both in the same state. We were at Grove Street in Beacon Hill instead of Randolph.

The area code would have made a difference in our initial search for the directions, but that was not entered. Fortunately, we were able to find the correct location within an hour.

How far forward should you go in a particular direction, you might ask? I believe that depends on the path that you are on and what is being accomplished by being on that path. If you are on the best path that would take you to the desired destination, keep on it. Keep going. Go the distance. Finish what you have started. If, however, you are on a path where the travel is tedious or you do not know or desire to go to the destination it is leading toward, it is time to stop and evaluate your situation.

It could be that something that you used to find fulfilling is no longer doing so. You are doing an activity but not finding much meaning. It is taking much of your time and resources, and you are not getting commensurate rewards, if any. While you might have some sentimental attachment because of your history, it no longer has your heart and passion. An important realization is that things have a shelf life. Ideas can outlive their true purpose. These

> *Things have a shelf life...Something that was good for yesterday might not always be good for tomorrow. A change is sometimes necessary.*

points of reduced capacity need to be acknowledged, and steps need to be taken to head in another direction that will lead to better outcomes. Something that was good for yesterday might not always be good for tomorrow. A change is sometimes necessary.

It might be time to change direction when one is not getting the desired results. Keeping things as they have always been and doing things the way you have always done is not the wisest decision if you desire improvement and continued results. You can become stuck doing something that once had meaning, was producing significant results, had many benefits, but is no longer doing so. That would be akin to going straight ahead when a turn might be needed. At such a point, you need to take time to do some evaluation. It might be time to go in another direction.

Go forward as far as your heart takes you. Go as far forward as you can with the given resources, opportunities, and capabilities afforded to you. Go as far forward as the returns outweigh the costs. When these are no longer true, do an evaluation to determine if something can be done to change the results positively while continuing along the same path or if a change of direction is needed.

Reflections and Notes

How have your perspectives been transformed based on the concepts that were highlighted in this chapter? How will you respond to the issues raised in this chapter as you go forward?

_____

_____

_____

_____

_____

WHO?

CHAPTER 5

WHO IS GOING FORWARD?

What came to mind when you saw the question, *"Who is going forward?"* Did you say to yourself, "Why is she even asking that question? Everyone knows the answer." I would then ask, "Do you really know the answer?"

At first glance, the question might appear to be rhetorical. It may even seem unnecessary. It is clear that whoever is stepping out or rolling along with eyes fixed on that target ahead is the protagonist of the story. Yet, there is much more intimated by the question than the identification of a physical being with a name. There is much more to the word *who*.

As I explore the *who* in this chapter, I will share a personal experience that has been instrumental in bringing to the fore thoughts on the subject. I recently completed a master's programme in an online modality. An important feature of online programmes is the development of a learning community. This is facilitated partly by establishing social presence as persons connect and interact with others through communication. In my programme, many of the courses required participants to introduce themselves in a video. Others asked us to share something about ourselves via a forum. I recall one such activity in which we were asked to introduce ourselves in a "What's in My Name" activity. Here's an excerpt from what I shared:

******

In the Shakespearean tragedy, *Romeo and Juliet*, the female character asked, "What's in a name?" as she reflected on the challenges she was experiencing with being with her beau because of the surname he bore. She eventually concluded that the name might not be that important since a rose, even if it were called something else, would smell just as sweet. While I understand the situation that led to Juliet's question, I am not sure that I agree fully with her conclusion. I believe that there is a lot in a name, and my name tells a unique story. Another name would not tell the same story.

I often begin presentations by sharing my name and reflecting on its importance. I am Keshawna Salmon-Ferguson. I use two surnames, my maiden name and my married name. I am proud of both aspects of my journey. I believe in honoring my past with all the sacrifices made by my parents to help me achieve what I have. Without the efforts of my parents, I would not have achieved what I did and would not have been in a position to meet my husband. Using my maiden name is my way of continuing to acknowledge and respect my past. My married name speaks to my current situation and honors the contributions my husband has made to my life. Both surnames mean a lot to me, and I desire them to be a part of my legacy, such that both my children have been given both names. I do not like it when persons do not use my maiden name, for example, in religious circles, because it is their view that once a female gets married, she should use her husband's surname only.

****

What did you see or hear about my name as you read this story? What do you understand about me? Did you see any significant social relationships? What impact have they had in shaping who I am? Do you understand anything about my thinking? How about my emotions? What have I displayed? Was there any spiritual indication? I know this was not in the story, but how tall do you think I am? Approximately how much do you think I weigh?

It would be interesting to hear your responses to see how closely they match up with who I am and what I believe I have displayed. Whatever your responses to these questions, they all speak to an aspect of who I am—the person behind the name.

I am a social being with physical attributes who experiences emotions and has thoughts as well as a spiritual perspective. These relate to the social, physical, emotional, cognitive, and spiritual aspects of a person. The interplay of all these aspects of a person is the essence of who he or she is.

Returning to the initial question of this chapter, to know *who* is going forward requires some understanding of the various aspects of the person. The person who is going forward represents more than a name. What are the social, emotional, physical, cognitive, and spiritual characteristics embodied in persons going forward? What are some useful considerations in each aspect to facilitate forward movement?

Social and Emotional Considerations

Psychologist Erik Erikson presented a theory of psychosocial development that shows how social interaction and relationships impact development across the lifespan. According to this theory, development occurs in stages. Importantly, each stage builds on the preceding stage and paves the way for the following periods of development. At each stage, there is a conflict that must be dealt with. Each conflict is centered around the development of a psychological quality or failure to develop that quality. If the conflict is successfully dealt with, persons emerge from the stage with psychological strengths and competence in certain areas of life. If they fail to deal with the conflicts effectively, they may not develop the essential skills needed for a strong

> *The person who is going forward represents more than a name. There are social, emotional, physical, cognitive, and spiritual characteristics embodied in the person going forward.*

sense of self and might have a sense of inadequacy in some aspects of development.

Based on Erikson's theory, newborns from birth to 18 months deal with trust versus mistrust. During this stage, newborns depend on others to take care of their basic needs, including feeding. If this is done effectively, the outcome is hope as trust is established. Erikson believed that early patterns of trust build the base for trust that is crucial for later social and emotional interactions. Children who learn to trust their caregivers will be more likely to form trusting relationships with others throughout their lives. Conversely, children raised by consistently unreliable, unpredictable parents who fail to meet their basic needs eventually develop a sense of mistrust. This sense of mistrust can cause them to become fearful, confused, and anxious in future relationships.

In toddlerhood, up until the age of three years, children struggle with autonomy versus shame and doubt as they undergo potty training. Other important events at this stage include gaining more control over food choices, toy preferences, and clothing selection. They ask, "Can I do this by myself or am I reliant on the help of others?" Children in this stage often feel the need to do things independently. Success in this stage results in the development of the will, which is the belief that one can act with intention. Otherwise, children who are shamed for their accidents, punished for making mistakes, or consistently encounter negative reactions could become doubtful and feel inadequate.

Preschoolers who have successfully completed the earlier two stages have a sense that the world is trustworthy and that they are able to act independently. They are now at the stage of engaging in exploration as they begin to assert power and control over their world by directing play and other social interactions. They do this as they plan activities, accomplish tasks, and face challenges. Children at this stage are beginning to exert more control over the things that impact their lives as they try things on their own and explore their own abilities. They are, however, conflicted between taking the initiative or feeling guilty for trying something that might be prohibited.

Where initiative is encouraged, children will develop purpose or drive. This occurs when children are given the freedom and encouragement to play and the chance to make choices while enforcing safe boundaries. Children whose efforts are stifled may begin to feel that their self-initiated efforts are a source of embarrassment and struggle to develop a sense of initiative and confidence in their abilities. To be successful at this stage, children should be encouraged to explore and helped to make appropriate choices. Children who successfully navigate this stage develop ambition and direction, leading to a meaningful social role. Those who fail to develop a sense of initiative at this stage may emerge with a fear of trying new things.

During the middle school years, as students navigate school life, they struggle with industry versus inferiority. At this stage, children enter the wider society beyond the family and need to learn to find their place. Social interactions with friends, peers, and teachers now play a crucial role in helping children develop pride in their accomplishments and abilities. As children are commended by parents and teachers as they perform increasingly complex tasks, they develop a feeling of competence and belief in their skills and abilities. They will become industrious, that is, productive and contributing members to society.

On the other hand, children who have caregivers who are discouraging or dismissive may feel ashamed of themselves and become overly dependent on others for help as they doubt their ability to be successful. They will continue to struggle in this stage and may develop low self-esteem resulting in inferiority. This inhibits productivity and fully contributing to society and the world as they will lack confidence. Confidence is linked to the feeling of competence. Children who struggle to develop a sense of competence may be less likely in later development to try new things or more likely to assume that their efforts will not measure up.

Erikson's fifth psychosocial stage takes place during the teenage years. This stage plays an important role in the development of a sense of personal identity that will continue to influence behaviour for the rest of one's life. The conflict to be resolved at this stage is identity versus confusion. Developing an identity or conscious sense of self is important. Adolescents establish a sense of self as they experiment with different roles, activities, and behaviours. Adolescents who successfully navigate this stage form a strong identity and develop a sense of direction in life. On the other hand, people who have not developed a personal identity tend to be unsure of who they are and where they fit, drift from one job or relationship to another, and could feel disappointed and confused about their place in life.

Erikson's sixth stage occurs between the ages of nineteen and forty, during the period of young adulthood. The major conflict at that stage is forming intimate, loving relationships with other people. The basic virtue to be achieved is love. Persons who successfully navigate this stage forge fulfilling relationships that play an important role in creating supportive social networks. Persons who struggle in this stage may find themselves lonely and isolated as they are not able to develop or share deep, intimate relationships. Things learned or achieved in earlier stages have an impact on success in this psychosocial stage. Findings suggest that having a strong sense of self is important in developing lasting relationships. People with a poor sense of self tend to have less committed relationships and are more likely to experience emotional isolation.[20]

The seventh psychosocial stage is concerned with persons in middle adulthood, ages 40–65, who are dealing with the conflict of generativity versus stagnation. The major events at this stage are parenthood and work. Persons in this stage are concerned with creating or nurturing things that will outlast them. They do so

> *Lack of hope, will, purpose, confidence, fidelity, love, care, and/or wisdom can impact on whether you go forward or how you move forward.*

through their parenting roles and other contributions to

---

[20] Mushtaq R, Shoib S, Shah T, Mushtaq S. Relationship between loneliness, psychiatric disorders and physical health? A review on the psychological aspects of loneliness. *J Clin Diagn Res.* 2014;8(9):WE01–WE4. doi:10.7860/JCDR/2014/10077.4828

society. Persons who are successful in this stage experience generativity. Generativity occurs as persons make their mark on the world by caring for others and creating and accomplishing things that make a difference. Persons who struggle in this stage might not feel like they are contributing to the world in the way they would like to and thus experience stagnation.

In the eighth psychosocial stage, older persons are focused on reflecting on their lives. As people look back on the events in their lives, if they are happy with their lives, they will feel a sense of fulfillment. Persons who feel proud of their accomplishments will have a sense of integrity. On the other hand, if they have regrets about the things they did or did not do, it could lead to bitterness and despair as they feel their life has been wasted. Successful completion of this final stage means looking back with few regrets and a general feeling of satisfaction.

How do you measure up on the psychosocial development scale? How trusting are you? Have you developed a sense of independence that makes you feel confident in launching out and exploring new initiatives, or do you keep doubting your ideas and abilities? How confident are you in your abilities and skills? Do you feel competent or incompetent? Have you resolved your identity such that you know who you are and what you desire and are guided by these in all that you do? What strong relationships do you have that serve as your supportive network? How have you facilitated or hindered such relationships? Do you feel like you are making a significant contribution to the world through your life and work? Do you have any regrets about the way your life is going or has gone? Please take the time to reflect on and answer these questions before you move on.

Your responses to these questions say much about *who* you are. Are you on the positive side related to every stage, or are there positive outcomes related to one or more stages that you have yet to achieve? Lack of development of the psychological qualities in respective stages can affect forward movement.

Indeed, lack of hope, will, purpose, confidence, fidelity, love, care, and/or wisdom can impact on whether you go forward or how you move forward. For example, if you lack confidence in your ability to do things on your own, you might find it hard to start a new venture, which might be the action needed to go forward. If this is so, although you might be very distressed working for an abusive and unreasonable boss and you are quite talented, you might not feel like you can make it if you were to launch out on your own. This lack of confidence has become a part of your psyche since you were constantly told "no" from childhood or that it would not work every time you attempted something.

Similarly, you could go forward by exploring a job or career path desired by other family members but not yourself. In such a situation, you might do enough to meet the minimum requirements but might not achieve excellence, a high degree of success, or even satisfaction if you are operating outside the zone of genius, as described by Gay Hendricks in *The Big Leap*. This could lead to stagnation instead of generativity as you are engaged in work that you do not really care about. Therefore, an important consideration in going forward is knowing yourself and being true to this knowledge.

It is important to know yourself and ultimately be guided by that truth in making decisions and taking action. In Hamlet, Shakespeare wrote, "This above all: to thine own self be true. And it must follow, as the night the day, thou canst not then be false to any man."

Who are you? What are your areas of psychological strength? What are your areas of weakness? Use your strengths to propel you forward and get help to deal with the areas in which you have lack. This is a part of accepting your reality.

In this section, you might realize that you have had some experiences that have shaped you negatively and will impact you going forward. Do not dwell too long on the negative happenings in the past (remember, you are encouraged to give yourself no more than 24 hours to brood). Accept that as part of your reality, take the necessary steps to deal with it, and go forward.

The psychological struggles that impact forward movement bring to mind the imagery of a parked vehicle. The vehicle might be parked for several reasons. If it is to be moved out of a parked position and put in motion, the action to be taken will be determined by the condition of the vehicle.

A vehicle that has all parts functioning but was just turned off as the driver temporarily parked to attend to other matters can simply be started with the touch of a button or the turn of a key. This represents actions that the driver—*you*—can take to move out of a parked position. If the area of psychological struggle is something you can deal with on your own as you encourage and speak to yourself positively or engage in other uplifting and transformative activity, then *do it*.

On the other hand, a vehicle could be parked because there is something that has malfunctioned. That vehicle might require that the driver get additional support to get it moving. For example, if a car battery has gone dead, calling roadside assistance to jumpstart the automobile will be necessary. That driver cannot get the car moving solely through his own efforts. In like manner, it is important to recognize when the psychological circumstances that have led to your immobility require that you get help to make a fresh start.

If you need help to overcome the psychosocial challenges that have hindered your forward movement, *get it*. Reach out to someone equipped to deal with the malfunction to be addressed; a counselor, therapist, mentor, minister, parent, supervisor, or other relevant professional. The help required might be from others or a spiritual source. People of faith can also reach out to God.

Doing what you can do on your own to deal with a situation and otherwise getting help where it is needed are principles to be applied to anything that needs to be done in life, as you seek to progress or move forward. There is something you can and need to do, *do it*! There are other things you need to get help with, *get it!*

Dealing with Fear

Another important consideration under the topic of emotional development is fear. People can experience various fears that inhibit them from moving forward or doing so in the most effective way.

Fear can be defined as an unpleasant emotion triggered by anticipation or awareness of danger, pain or harm. It is a basic human emotion that helps to protect us. Fear alerts us to danger and prepares us to deal with it through a flight or fight response.

People develop unnecessary fears, usually through negative experiences that trigger a fear reaction. Such experiences could include those related to Erikson's psychosocial stages of development, as previously explained. Some persons can experience intense fear that is not associated with any single event.

Fear, like other emotions, can be experienced in degrees. Depending on the situation and person, it can be mild, moderate, or intense. People fear things or situations that make them feel unsafe or unsure. As such, they tend to avoid the situation or things they fear.

Fear can be healthy or unhealthy. When fear is healthy, it cautions a person to stay safe around something that could indeed be dangerous. In such a situation, you appropriately avoid a real threat. On the other hand, when someone has a fear that causes more caution than is necessary in the situation, that fear is unhealthy. Avoiding something that does not pose a real threat could be disadvantageous. Energy is wasted in

> *As you encounter challenges in going forward, including dealing with fear, do what you can and get help to do what you can't.*

fueling the fear, and alternatively, energy might not be used to engage in an activity that could prove useful because of the fear.

Fear that is impacting your progress needs to be dealt with. It is important to face and overcome the fear. It takes a willingness to *admit* that one has a fear, a *belief* that it is possible to have another reaction or response to the situation that has triggered the fear, and a *commitment* to taking the necessary steps to overcome the fear. I call this the ABC of overcoming. I believe this principle can be applied to dealing with fear or any other challenge one needs to overcome:

> **A**ccept the current reality.
> **B**elieve in a new possibility.
> **C**ommit to transformative activity.

In this process of dealing with and overcoming fear, you are reminded to do what you can and get help to do what you can't.

Physical Considerations

Whether walking or rolling along in a wheelchair, the act of movement involves a physical component. Any tangible or intangible action in the process of moving forward necessitates a physical being—a body—an object. Therefore, consideration must also be given to the person's physical aspects in looking at the *who* in moving forward.

It is already seen that one's physical state will determine the manner of movement possible. That is, while persons who are non-disabled can use their legs for movement, persons with a physical disability might require the use of a wheelchair, crutches, walkers, or other mobility aids. Besides issues related to physical ability, other health issues have implications for moving forward. Consideration must be given to one's physical and mental state in the process of moving forward.

I had a recent personal experience that has made me more aware of the real impact of health on moving forward. I got a rude awakening when, after a routine pap smear, I was alerted to a major cancer-related situation in my reproductive system that required immediate surgery. I am grateful for God's intervention and the help of the doctors who have enabled me to have additional time to fulfil my purpose. Without that, I might not have been able to move forward even in writing this book. I can no longer take life and health for granted. I strongly encourage others to do the same.

Visit your doctor regularly and do routine checks even if you feel okay. Pay attention to signs and symptoms in your body. Do not ignore the pain. Even if you think you can bear it, do so but investigate to determine if there might be any underlying conditions that require treatment. Your forward journey could be shortened by ill health and what some might describe as untimely death.

Going forward could become more challenging if you are not well as you deal with pain and other symptoms. There are some physical conditions that are unavoidable, such as congenital defects and disorders over which one has no control. That is a limiting cap that one must deal with. There are, however, other conditions over which you have control. Do what you can to control them.

You might not have a fever or any visible signs of illness, but how healthy are you? What are your vitals? What's your blood pressure reading? How is your blood sugar level? Do not take it for granted that because you are not sick or rather not showing signs of illness that you are well. Things could be happening inside the body that you are not aware of. According to the World Health Organization (WHO), "Health is a state of complete physical, mental, and social well-being and not merely the absence of disease or infirmity."[21] Do the necessary health checks recommended at your age and based on your family history, even if you are not feeling unwell or sick.

Up to the time I wrote this section, my father's life had been extended by thirteen years because he chose to do prostate examinations, given the history of prostate cancer in his family. He was not showing visible signs of illness, but all was not well in his body. The cancer was caught early, and he was able to have his prostate gland removed through surgery.

> *Health is a state of complete physical, mental, and social well-being and not merely the absence of disease or infirmity.* —*World Health Organization*

Yes, he eventually died from some other condition, but having

---

[21] Retrieved from WHO website at
https://www.who.int/about/governance/constitution#:~:text=Health%20is%20a%20state%20of,belief%2C%20economic%20or%20social%20condi tion.

over a decade of life to move forward in his work and ministry is something to be grateful for. Understanding and dealing with who you are physically is a part of moving forward.

Depending on your health status, there are things you might or might not be able to do in seeking to move forward. Understanding this reality about your physical status is useful. The actions you can take will be informed in some ways by your physical state. It is important to know what you can possibly do, how much you can handle, and for how long.

To move forward and keep moving forward requires endurance—doing what needs to be done for the long haul. How long will you be able to keep at what you are doing or need to do to move forward? Might you need to get into better shape physically, check on major organs, or work on weight reduction? If any of these is a concern for you, take the necessary precautions and treatment for diseases that are treatable. Illnesses and diseases affect one's ability to function and can hamper forward movement.

Your physical health will determine the pace at which you are able to move. Know your health status and limitations and work accordingly. Do not take on more than you can reasonably handle physically. Know when to say no. Know how far and how fast you can go. Set reasonable limits and timelines as you go forward. Accept what you can and cannot do, given your physical situation.

Demands will be placed on the body to perform the necessary actions to go forward. You will need to determine if you can physically handle all the things required to be done. What adjustments might you need to make to have the physical capacity to move forward? Remember, if there is something you can do, do it!

Remember that rest is important. Make time for rest in your activities as you move forward. Yes, take time to rejuvenate and recuperate. Your body will thank you.

Cognitive Considerations

I will begin this section by making a statement based on my observations and personal experience. Where the physical body is capable, and the resources are available, one is only limited by thoughts in achieving forward motion. Your cognitions thus play a significant role in the actions that are taken or not taken that facilitate or otherwise prevent forward movement.

I have seen children who have great intellectual capacity with parents who make the effort to provide the necessary help and support for them. However, those children fail to advance as much as they can scholastically. In many instances, such failure is due to the children's ideas about what is or isn't important, which in turn drives what they do and the efforts they make to achieve. In such cases, what the children believe determine what they achieve.

You cannot push a child or person to work to achieve something that he or she has not accepted is possible or worthwhile. This brings two words to mind—efficacy and meaning. To take an action that will cause you to advance in some area requires that you believe in your ability to satisfactorily perform the task to produce the desired result.

This is self-efficacy. It is your belief in your ability to succeed in a particular situation.

Bringing self-efficacy into the previous scenario of the child with academic concerns, all the parents' efforts to have the child receive additional tutoring and provide relevant materials will not result in the

Where the physical body is capable and the resources are available, one is only limited by thoughts in achieving forward motion.

child doing well if the child does not believe that he or she can do well in the subject. The child's limiting thoughts will affect the effort expended and, to a great extent, what is achieved.

In a similar manner, if you do not believe that some action on your part will produce desirable results, you might be reluctant to take such actions. A very important aspect of moving forward is, therefore, your thoughts. You cannot move beyond what you believe is possible. I dare say that what you see is what you get. What you think is what you will achieve. You will not go further than your thoughts. Paul Martinelli says, "You create your life through your thinking." What are you thinking?

Yes, dealing with the primary *who* in the story will require dealing with your thoughts, whether limiting or facilitating. What do you think you can or cannot do? To move forward requires more than the physical and emotional aspects. One of the first things that need to be addressed is cognitive capacity, which is dealing with the self.

GO FORWARD: YOUR PERSONAL GUIDE

Some questions you might be asking directly or indirectly—the answers to which will impact your forward motion—are the following:

- Do I really believe it is possible to go forward?
- Do I really believe it is possible to go forward in that area?
- Do I really want to go forward, or am I more comfortable with what is tried and proven?
- Am I willing to put out the effort required to move forward?
- Do I believe it is worth moving forward?
- How much effort should I invest, and what if it doesn't work out?
- Can I do it on my own, or do I need help?
- What shape am I in to move forward? Am I able to handle it?
- What resources do I have—or will I need—to move forward? Do I have them or can I afford it?

Your answers to these questions constitute your belief and will determine if you take the necessary steps to move forward. I strongly recommend that you work through these and related questions as you take steps to move forward. Again, get help where necessary to answer these questions.

Before I close this section, I must also deal with the matter of meaning. While you can believe in your ability to carry out a task, the impetus to undertake the task is tied to the meaning that the task has for you. In other words, while you recognize that you have the ability to do something, the value, importance, or meaning the thing has for you will determine whether you think it is worth expending the effort to take the action.

Returning to the scenario of the teenager in high school, a child might know and believe in his ability but fail to exert the energy that parents would desire or expect to get higher grades because that might not be important to the child. Getting the highest grades possible commensurate with the child's ability might be important to the parent but not considered valuable or significant to the child. The child might, therefore, only expend just enough to pass but not enough to get the A because that is not meaningful for him or her.

Like high school students, adults also have to contend with doing things they consider meaningful. If you are to advance, it is important to know what you value, what is important, or what has meaning for you. It will be hard to move forward doing something that you do not value or that does not have much meaning for you. Doing things that are not meaningful will be akin to performing chores. There will be little enjoyment and could be even

> *If what you say is not what you see, it is very possible that you will not achieve what you say.*

burdensome. Therefore, you are encouraged to find what is meaningful for you and take the necessary steps to move forward.

You can usually see yourself in the role when something has meaning for you. You see yourself experiencing that thing,

133

and it bringing pleasure or some form of fulfilment. Otherwise, you will be like the child who does not find personal meaning in getting an A and so does not strive for that grade. I was like that child.

Although medicine is considered to be a great career and a profession that the intellectually able are encouraged to strive for, that profession did not have much meaning for me. I cannot remember picturing myself walking around attending to sick patients in a medical setting. I really did not see myself being a doctor. In fact, I was repulsed by hospitals and medical situations. Can I tell you, though, that I saw myself talking to people and helping them to learn and think differently? I was fascinated with the mind. I enjoyed going down to Bellevue Hospital as the patients with mental health issues did not turn me off, but I would puke at the smell of other hospitals.

What had meaning for me was being a psychologist and not a medical doctor. Understanding this aspect of who I am has been important in me moving forward into something that would give fulfilment and help me to achieve significance. In my subconscious, what I was seeing was what I was thinking about, and what I was thinking was what really had meaning for me, not necessarily what I was saying.

If you asked at the end of sixth form what I wanted to pursue as a career, I most certainly would have said medicine. That, however, was what others were seeing and thinking about for me, which I was obediently repeating and not what I was seeing or truly thinking deep on the inside for myself. What I was saying did not line up with what I was seeing. I realize that if what you say is not what you see, it is very possible that you will not achieve what you say.

What do you see? That is revealing something about what has meaning for you. Use what you see, which is the basis for what you think, as a guidepost for moving forward. Look at what you have been saying about the direction in which you want to go. Does what you are saying match up with what you are seeing and thinking? If not, that could cause you to be stuck or not make significant progress in the direction you have been attempting to go.

You should not forget that the person going forward has thoughts and feelings, which can create a drive that propels movement or produce inertia that reduces movement. Movement toward what you see is more likely to propel you forward than trying to create a dream out of something you do not envision.

Reflections and Notes

How have your perspectives been transformed based on the concepts that were highlighted in this chapter? Who are you, how are you, what has meaning for you, and how do these guide you in moving forward?

_____

_____

_____

_____

_____

CHAPTER 6

WHO DO I NEED AS I MOVE FORWARD?

In the previous chapter, the emphasis was on the protagonist in the story. However, I have yet to encounter a story involving only one character. Albeit one character might be portrayed or highlighted in the rendition of the story; that main character never exists on his/her own. Who the character is and what he or she does is always dependent on some association with others. A section on who is involved when going forward would, therefore, not be complete without considering other characters and players in the story. The opening and closing credits are significant in a production.

It is interesting that having had some life-changing experiences, a good friend and I recently dubbed the next phase of our lives the *second season premiere* as we intentionally set out to play starring roles in the new chapter of our lives. The previous chapter was certainly a hybrid genre with many mysteries, much drama, some horrors, with a few scenes of comedy and romance. As we move from success to significance as our stories unfold, I envision there will still be some mysteries, but I hope there will be less drama and horrors, with an increase in romance and adventure.

One must also consider the production team, the cast, and the crew essential for the production. The star cannot produce the show by him/herself. Be it many or few, others will play some role in the production being completed. There are three roles that I would like to focus on in the going forward—next phase of life production. These are the scriptwriters, directors, and supporting characters.

Scriptwriters

I contend that there can be no story or production without the scriptwriter. The scriptwriter writes the material that will be performed, including creating the characters, writing believable dialogue, and engaging plots. The scriptwriter must demonstrate creativity in developing original ideas and writing satisfying endings to the story developed. Depending on the origins and nature of the work, there can be one or more scriptwriters, and a scriptwriter might also act in the production that he or she has written.

It is my belief that the lives of human beings are originally scripted by the creator and designer, God. Humans ultimately partner with God in developing the details of the scripts that unfold in the story of their lives. It is important, therefore, to understand God's intent for one's life, such that the life that evolves will ultimately be in accord with the original purpose and design.

Therefore, as you seek to move forward and make advancements to fulfill purpose, it is critical that communication is made with God. This can be done through prayer, meditation, and reflection on God's Word as outlined in the Scriptures or otherwise revealed. God speaks through these and other means to give information and clarity about various aspects of life. Lack of awareness of your true state and clarity about the direction in which you should go could lead to you being stuck in the story and simply repeating the same scenario every day for a long time as in Groundhog Day.

Have you found yourself in a time loop? Have you had the same experiences daily for a little while now? Do you keep returning to the same point you should have passed some time ago? Do you keep making the same mistakes that you should have overcome by now? Communication with the chief scriptwriter could help to take you out of the time loop. Let him know what you are experiencing and what you desire to understand so you can be guided on how to continue adding to the script instead of having that scene on a repeat loop.

You need to partner with God in continuing to add to the script of your life in order to move forward. You will encounter significant challenges if you try to write the script alone. Only God, the Creator, knows the overall plot. However, as co-scriptwriters, humans work with God to determine how the various scenes will unfold.

Directors

Sometimes, the act of going forward begins with a directive given by someone else to do so. This can be seen in armed forces, where officers give commands to members. The members are expected to follow the directives of the commander. While life is not quite like the armed forces, there are times when leaders and others who have some influence in your life will do well to give you some instruction to go forward, thereby acting as commanders. This role could be equated to a director who holds the creative vision and ultimately directs the making of the production as the actors and technical crew are guided to capture the vision of the script. Directors interpret scripts and turn them into a creative vision for the show.

In a production, the director can be a distinct individual with no other role. Sometimes, the director can be the scriptwriter or even an actor. Given the multifaceted nature of our lives, there will likely be more than one director in this life production. Firstly, God, the main scriptwriter with supernatural knowledge, wisdom, and power, would make the best director. It is prudent to accord Him that role to ensure the best possible outcomes.

As director, there are instructions that God will give to get the best performance and to ensure that the technical aspects are in place to facilitate a great production. People would do well to listen to and obey God-given instructions to move them forward in various aspects of their lives. In this regard, you are encouraged to conduct a self-examination to determine the extent to which you seek after and receive instructions from God about actions to be taken in regard to your life. Another consideration is the extent to which God-given directives have been heeded. A gap in these areas could mess up the production, requiring re-takes. The more re-takes required, the longer it will be before the production is completed. Don't take longer than you need to advance because of your own stubbornness or disobedience. Don't stand in your own way of going forward. Who is directing your life production?

Besides God, there can be other directors in your life. There are others who have a vision of some aspect of the script and can give directives that will see the vision played out in your life. There are times when others see abilities, potential, and possibilities that you do not see and would serve you well to direct you to take action in those aspects of your life. Some persons need directors to help them to move forward. They need someone to create a spark that will ignite their inner passions to work at something that will propel them forward.

My husband served as a catalyst in this way to push me forward in the area of writing. I needed to go forward as an author but I required a jolt. My husband's words of challenge and encouragement did it. His loving support throughout the process removed some barriers that had kept me in a place of non-achievement, a place where my dream was buried—not fully acknowledged—and even seemed daunting. His matter-of-fact directive to write the book was not a question asking me to see if it is something I would like to think about and act on if I felt it was a good way to go. It was an affirmation of what he believed to be an ability that I have that needed full expression and that I could reasonably accomplish. Any doubts I had about writing were dispelled in that moment. I forthwith set to the task of writing the book. I am now living out that part of the script of my life—being an author.

As you look out for directors in your life, consider what persons of significance and influence have said to you about some aspect of your life that you might not have considered or that you could give more attention to. What have your children said to you about something that you could do but you have not given much thought because it is only coming from a child? What aspect of your work has your boss commented on that gives an indication of the area in which you should focus for further training or for doing your own business? What traits or abilities have your friends pointed out that you have but to which you have not given much thought?

There are persons in your life who mean you well and to whom you should listen as they point you to ideas and things that will facilitate your advancement if you pay attention to them. It will not always be easy to listen to what others say, especially when the directive requires you to step outside of your comfort zone or stretch and do things that you consider hard or when what is said triggers some raw emotions. It is also sometimes challenging to consider what is said by others when the full meaning and results are not apparent. However, it is always worth considering the ideas shared by others. Evaluate what is shared to find the truth, then act on it. Knowing the truth and acting on that truth will set one free (see John 8:32).

Are you someone who needs a director, or will you serve as a director for others to move forward? There are some of us whose advancement is wrapped up in how we help others to go forward. We are directors. People need our help to move forward. We need to play our role. This is part of understanding our *why*, a subject that will be discussed in a subsequent chapter.

As a director, your voice in the ears of those you are sent to help commands attention that will get them moving. There is a power that you have in their lives and/or respect they have for you that makes this possible. Use that power to help them to go forward. You might have legitimate power based on your status or formal job authority. You might have expert power based on others' perception of your competence. You might have information power by possessing knowledge that others want and need, or you might just have referent power based on how others identify with you or the liking they have for you. Director, use whatever power you have to lift or push others to a higher level. Help them go forward so you, too, can go forward as you seek to fulfill your own purpose. According to Zig Ziglar, if you help enough other people get what they want, you will get what you want.

The power you have as a director is embedded in the leadership role associated with such a position. Lifting, pushing, motivating, or inspiring others to change means influencing their movement to another level or position. The process of influencing others is about leadership. John Maxwell, the guru on the subject, says, "Leadership is influence, nothing more, nothing less." Leadership does not require one to have a title or a named position. It only necessitates that you recognize the power you have to impact others and use that power to the best of your ability to influence positive change in others. Effective directors are great leaders. You are encouraged to recognize and develop the leadership potential that you possess to effectively help in directing your own life and that of others.

Directors, do not be swayed by the doubts, disbelief, and fears of those you are sent to direct. Be confident in what you are called to do and in the potential that others have. Keep giving directives with loving support as you help others to move forward.

It is useful to have a growth mindset, as proposed by Carol Dweck. This mindset is based on the belief that qualities that lead to success can be cultivated. This is opposed to having a fixed mindset where one sees qualities as unchangeable and situations as fixed, and this causes one not to engage with life in the way one ought to. The growth mindset, on the other hand, creates a passion for learning and growing, which propels one forward.

Both directors and persons who are to move forward must have a growth mindset if advancement is to occur. The director needs to see growth potential in the person being directed, and the person being directed needs to believe that growth is possible. This is captured in what Dweck describes as the "power of yet." There is always something else yet to be achieved or attained as one seeks to learn and grow, even from challenges. Do you have a fixed or a growth mindset? A growth mindset is essential for moving forward.

Supporting Characters

In his book *Outliers*, Malcolm Gladwell explains how social and cultural characteristics contribute to the success of extremely successful people. Gladwell shows that success takes more than individual characteristics, merit, and hard work. Success also depends on people receiving crucial help or being in the right place at the right time. That crucial help comes from others. Indeed, it is true that no man is an island.

People need all kinds of help and support as they seek to advance. There is a need for instrumental support in the form of tangible aid and service. There are things that others need to physically do or provide to facilitate someone moving forward. One, for example, might need someone to keep a child while she goes to take up a job that will provide some resources for her to be less dependent on an abusive partner. Kind words from family and friends will not be enough to help her deal with and move beyond the debilitating situation. Instrumental support is required. Some supportive action is needed from others, not just words.

I am reminded of Scriptures that admonish believers that the love of God is demonstrated in His followers by the tangible ways in which they support others. James 2:15-16 says: *"Suppose a brother or a sister is without clothes and daily food. If one of you says to them, "Go in peace; keep warm and well fed," but does nothing about their physical needs, what good is it?" (NIV)*. Likewise, 1 John 3:17–18 states: *"But if anyone has the world's goods and sees his brother in need, yet closes his heart against him, how does God's love abide in him? Little children, let us not love in word or talk but in deed and in truth." (ESV)*. Persons guided by these scriptures and the Word of God in general will recognize the importance of providing tangible support to others as they help people take care of their needs to move to a better place—go forward.

Some people have some of the things that others need to get out of the place they are to move forward to a better place. These people are destiny helpers. In a presentation on the topic *Destiny Helpers and Destiny Killers*, Deaconess O. Balogun of The Redeemed Christian Church of God, Abuja shared some characteristics of destiny helpers and what they do. [22]

> A mistake many people make is trying to do things alone. You are weakest when you are alone.

She says destiny helpers are strategically positioned to help you arrive at your destiny. God ordains these people to assist you to move forward into your destiny, as they share physical and other resources, experiences, and wisdom, among other things. They remove barriers, help to navigate obstacles, fight on your behalf, and/or use their networks to open up opportunities as they add value to the person being helped.

I have been fortunate to experience the help and support of destiny helpers as I have sought to advance in various aspects of my life. This book's completion is largely due to the support of destiny helpers in my life. Thanks to my friend, Donna-Marie Rowe, who connected me with author and publisher, Crystal Daye, who provided the necessary tools to navigate the world of writing and publishing. Yes, Donna-Marie is a connector, an enabler, and my accountability partner. She has been a critical supporter on my journey as a

---

[22] Retrieved from https://rccghouseoffruits.wordpress.com/2019/11/24/destiny-helpers-and-destiny-killers/

parent, entrepreneur, minister of the gospel of Christ, and a person in general. Together, we are *on the grow*. She has made many suggestions, shared ideas, given recommendations, opened doors, offered correction, and pointed me in the right direction on numerous occasions.

Who do you have in your life that resembles my husband, Trevor, my sister friend, Donna, and my coach, Crystal—people who encourage you, affirm you, help you overcome doubts, provide you with tools for success, and generally help you to move forward in some area of your life? Identify and acknowledge these people and their importance in your life. A mistake many people make is trying to do things alone.

I once read a story about a young girl and her father who were walking along a path when they came across a large tree branch on the ground. The young girl, eager to get ahead, and wanting to be industrious even as she sought to deal with challenges, asked her father if he thought she could move the branch. Her father's reply was that she could move the branch if she could use all her strength. With that assurance, the young girl tried her best to lift the branch but could not move it.

She became disappointed at her failed attempt and expressed this to her father, who kept encouraging her to try again with all her strength. The girl continued to try hard but just could not move the branch. She finally cried out in desperation, saying, "I cannot do it!" Her father replied, "I advised you to use *all your strength*. You did not ask for my help."

Indeed, the girl's understanding of what was her strength was limited. She saw this as existing only in herself and her individual efforts. She had an independence perspective. However, she failed to realize that some of her strength, yes, *her* strength, lay in the human and other resources that are available, which she could tap into to accomplish the task. It required an interdependent perspective.

In my role as counsellor, I often find that persons are distressed and stuck in a place of pain and despair because they fail to get the necessary help to deal with problem situations. People are sometimes laden with overwhelming issues that they carry on their own and struggle under the weight of the load they bear, usually with significant consequences. Abuse victims are warned not to tell anyone and believe the lie that the pain must be borne alone. Others do not feel it is okay to ask for advice on dealing with a difficult task as such an act diminishes them, and thus, they continue to struggle to the point of breaking. The relief only comes after they are willing to invite others into the process to give the necessary support.

Moving forward in the best possible way will mean recognizing that you will not be able to accomplish everything based on your strengths. The strength of the collective can be your power to move forward. People who end up committing suicide have not tapped into this power and have been limited by the independence perspective. Yes, something may be daunting when dealt with alone, but there is power in numbers. Someone else helping you with the same load will make it lighter and easier to manage.

A quote attributed to Lena Horne is quite apt with respect to how one deals with loads. It says, "It is not the load that breaks you down, it's the way you carry it." Your attitude towards dealing with a challenging situation makes the difference in how you are affected by and how you get over the situation. Yes, the load might not all be moved in one go, but the important thing is that it can be moved and dealt with; the situation can change little by little over time with help, available tools and resources, human, and others.

Don't underestimate the power of *we*. To move forward, there is a need for a paradigm shift from the inadequacy of <u>me</u> to the power of <u>we</u>. Change the limiting independence perspective to an interdependence paradigm that will help you to go beyond.

Don't be afraid to ask for help and to be vulnerable. Be willing to take council. Share your dreams and aspirations with destiny helpers. You are weakest when you are alone. You are more easily broken by your situations when you are alone. Consider the wisdom of Solomon in Ecclesiastes 4:12, who advises that *"A person standing alone can be attacked and defeated, but two can stand back-to-back and conquer. Three are even better, for a three-braided cord is not easily broken."* (NLT). Do not be afraid to ask for and accept help. Override your pride.

> *To move forward, there is a need for a paradigm shift from the inadequacy of me to the power of <u>we</u>. Change the limiting independence perspective to an interdependence paradigm that will help you to go beyond.*

Another type of support that someone might need to move forward is informational support. People need the right information to take the right action to move forward.

Sometimes, it is more important to make contact with the right people who have the information you need to put you on the right path to achieving success, than to spend many hours slaving over an idea on your own. We often waste time doing unnecessary things or not doing the things we should be doing to move us in the right direction because we lack information. Persons who are serious about moving forward would do well to seek out and get information from others who know and have experience in the area in which they desire to venture. Never feel that you are above getting advice and suggestions from others as you work out the specific details of moving forward.

My father once told me, "It is a fool who learns everything from his own mistakes, and you are no fool." I have found wisdom in this statement as I have sought to navigate various situations in my youth and continue to find it relevant in moving forward in several areas of life. Learning from others vicariously as one observes their behaviours and the consequences, or directly as they share experiences and ideas, is a trait to be encouraged. Trying to do it all on one's own is imprudent. Why waste time and energy doing something that has already been done and making mistakes that have already been made when there are new things to be experienced and explored to advance all concerned?

I challenge you, like I have been challenged, not to waste another day in your life. Read all the material you can, talk to all the people you can, participate in all the activities you can, to find out all you can, to move forward as best and as fast as you can. Strive to do your best and be your best to ensure you achieve the most as you move forward. This will include listening to others and getting support from others in the process.

One valuable way to get support from others is through mentorship. The leadership expert and my coach and mentor, John Maxwell, shared that mentorship has been the number one way in which he has grown personally. He says, "You will never get the best answer if you rely only on yourself for the answer." If you desire to find the best answers to help you move forward in some area of your life, seek out mentors. Find others who know what you need to know in the area where you desire to grow and learn from them.

In the process of mentorship, the mentor shares wisdom learned from his or her life with another, becoming a fountain of assets and knowledge. As you learn from the mentor, the information learned should be used to create new things in yourself. Thereafter, the wise mentee takes action based on this learning. It is this action that will move you forward.

I have benefitted from mentorship in my own life as I transitioned from being a full-time academic and educational administrator to becoming an entrepreneur. There was a call to stretch—a call to move into an area that would combine all the things that had deep meaning for me into an entity that would help me achieve success and significance. I, however, had many questions, doubts, and fears. And, of course, the high C in me needed to know the details of how exactly this thing would work so that I could feel comfortable taking on the challenge.

I had stepped out of the boat but was still holding onto the sides, wanting to but not quite wanting to take the full plunge into the ocean of possibilities. After a soul-stirring charge from my mentor, John Maxwell, at an International Maxwell Conference to "just say YES," I made a decision to fully accept the challenge to say yes to entrepreneurship and all the associated possibilities as I utilize my strengths and abilities to add value to others. Becoming part of the John Maxwell certified team, where I have mentors like John Maxwell, Chris Robinson, Mark Cole, Valorie Burton, and Roddy Galbraith, has been a phenomenal growth experience in helping me move forward. I am able to get my questions answered, and my fears have been allayed as I receive information, coaching, and guidance about how to go forward in this phase of my journey.

> *Find others who know what you need to know in the area where you desire to grow and learn from them.*

I have no doubt that as I progress, I will find additional mentors. Their experience and wisdom will be useful for my growth and development in those new dimensions of my life to which I will attain. As you move forward, be prepared to deal with yourself and engage with others to ensure that the most is achieved on the journey. Find mentors, identify destiny helpers, listen to your directors as you seek to write the most beautiful story of your life.

Reflections and Notes

How have your perspectives been transformed based on the concepts that were highlighted in this chapter? Who are the people that you need to support you in moving forward? What will you do to find such people, and how will you use their help?

_____

_____

_____

_____

_____

_____

_____

_____

_____

_____

_____

_____

_____

_____

_____

_____

WHEN?

CHAPTER 7

WHEN DO I GO FORWARD?

I agree that I need to move from where I am to another place in my career, relationships, spirituality, or some other aspect of my life. Yes, I should go forward, but when should I do this? What is the right time to take the step? How do I know when it is the right time to move forward? What needs to be in place for me to move forward? These are all important questions to be answered.

In response to these questions, I contend that it is always the right time to do the right thing. You always advance when you do the right thing. Every moment that you are alive presents an opportunity to do something. What you do in each moment will determine whether or not you advance. It is important to do the right thing in each moment.

In other words, from the moment that a decision is made to move forward, there is always something that can be done to advance. We are all given 24 hours each day, equivalent to 1440 minutes or 86,400 seconds. If we use a second as the span of time with which we are concerned, or a moment, we have

86,400 opportunities to do the right thing—something that moves us forward each day.

The use of time is a serious matter. Too many people waste time doing unimportant things that keep them in the same place or even cause them to regress instead of moving forward.

> *It is always the right time to do the right thing.*

To do what is right in each moment, in other words, doing what is important requires an inner drive. It requires overcoming inertia. It requires doing something that gets you beyond the state of being stuck or out of paralysis.

I think this matter of paralysis or inertia is worth exploring in some detail in this section. Quite often, there is the desire to move forward, but something stands in the way that hinders movement. Such blockage can result from external forces, or they can be internal.

Recognizing the blockage is an important first step in doing what needs to be done to move forward. An analysis of the situation is necessary. What about the situation that is external to self that is impacting your movement? What are the conditions within you that are affecting movement? It is important to tell yourself the truth.

Part of that truth will mean accepting things about yourself that are inhibitory to movement as well as external contributing factors. The psychology of attribution helps us realize that it is easier to attribute the cause of negative situations to external factors than to acknowledge internal causes. It might be simple to identify external inhibitory factors while disregarding even more consequential internal inhibitory factors that have led to paralysis.

Denial, another concept in psychology, is also relevant here. It is the refusal to perceive that painful facts exist. Denial is a type of defense mechanism, that is, a strategy used to cope with distressing feelings to avoid the anxiety associated with dealing with the fact. Denial can involve not acknowledging a fact—the reality or denying the consequences of the reality.

Not acknowledging the existence of or the effects of either external or internal factors causing paralysis is an act of denial. It will be important to come to terms with such reality to be able to get out of the state of paralysis and start moving as soon as possible. You are cautioned to be open and honest in reflecting on the circumstances impacting movement at any moment.

Dealing with External Factors

External inhibitory factors can be many and varied, including the attitudes and actions of others. To deal with these factors, you must do what is within your power to reach out to others, using appropriate means to persuade them to employ alternate actions in your favour.

Wishing things are not how they are will not change them. We cannot wish things away. You need to take action in your own best interest. You must play an active role in your progress by talking, writing, praying, and/or doing something else to change the situation. This you must do, while always being cognizant that the response of others is out of your control.

Intervention will sometimes result in others making adjustments that remove blockages to your movement. When this occurs, you should be grateful and make effective use of the opportunity presented to advance.

What do you do when the external factors or factors you have no control over do not shift in your favour? Some people here become paralyzed, unable to move. You must overcome such paralysis to take important action in each moment so as not to remain stuck.

When faced with any situation, a useful approach is to consider all the possibilities. There is always another way. Because you do not yet perceive that other way, it does not mean it doesn't exist. A way to deal with the situation can be found if you seek hard enough and long enough with the right methods and tools.

> *The longer you put off doing the right thing, the longer it takes to move forward.*

Always remember that an important part of the strategy should be the inclusion of others—human and supernatural. With the all-powerful God as the scriptwriter and director, edits can be made to any aspect of the script for a totally unexpected outcome. With the script in the hands of the director, anything is possible.

To become unstuck, you must believe that there is another possibility other than your current state and reach toward that other state of being. To get out of a state of paralysis, you must envision another possibility for behaving and move towards that possibility.

Envisioning other possibilities will require taking time to think. Take time to explore options. Take time to brainstorm. It requires taking what Juliet Funt in *A Minute to Think* describes as a strategic pause; when one stops to think in order to come up with new approaches to solve problems.

This strategic pause should involve asking questions to determine assets that can be explored and risks that need to be reduced. For example, based on the R's of high-value work, the P's of low-value work, and the M's of capacity management, as suggested by Juliet Funt, one could ask:

- What else can be done to increase my revenue, my reputation, the rewards I get from what I do, and/or my readiness to effectively deal with the situations I encounter?

- What are the things that are causing me to be panicking, pandering to please others, padding to make things look better than they really are, and/or overly driven by procedure, and what can I do to reduce them?

- What can I do to increase manpower, have more money, get more time, and/or make things of a magnitude that is manageable?

The answers to these questions present possibilities to be explored. If you find it challenging to come up with the answers by yourself, bring others into the possibilities—finding conversation.

What are the possibilities? What are the options for dealing with that inhibitory factor? After careful consideration, prayer, and deliberation, which option(s) among the possibilities will you choose? You must make a decision and take the necessary action. Don't put it off. Do it now.

Remember that procrastination is the thief of time. The longer you put off doing the right thing, the longer it takes to move forward. Every moment something remains undone, time is lost and can never be regained. This means that less time remains to do the right thing and experience the rewards of doing so.

Using every moment wisely is one way to move forward. Every moment that is not spent in pursuit of something that results in advancement is a wasted moment. You, therefore, must become purposeful about how each moment is spent. Be deliberate about using each moment to engage in an activity geared towards fulfilling some purpose—doing something that moves you forward in some aspect of life.

This attitude or approach to living will require constant self-evaluation. In what way(s) do you desire to move forward? How are your actions in each moment facilitating that forward movement? Your honest response to these questions will reveal whether your actions are indeed moving you forward or keeping you in a place of paralysis.

The right thing might be a hard thing to do. You will need to muster all the courage to do that hard thing while it is the right thing. This will require dealing with some internal inhibitory factors, including debilitating and unhealthy thoughts and feelings. These will be considered later in the chapter.

As you move forward, something else must be said about dealing with external factors. There are times when the circumstances leave you in a situation where previous thoughts and plans are no longer feasible. That could present a situation where you get stuck if you are beholden to moving only with the idea as it was originally structured. This, however, does not have to be.

> *Work with your circumstances to achieve desirable outcomes. You can't always determine your circumstances, but you can choose how to respond to them.*

It might require rethinking the plan, revising the goal, or doing something else that will get you moving. Don't get so tied to one plan or idea that you are not able to recognize when you might need to consider another option to move forward.

Be open to new possibilities and other ways of achieving your ultimate vision. Some would say, don't let your circumstances dictate your outcome. I would go further to say work with your circumstances to achieve desirable outcomes. We can't always determine or change our circumstances. We can, however, choose how we respond to them.

After you have placed effort into trying to change your circumstances, it is important to realize when that effort should be directed elsewhere. You must be open to considering other possibilities when things do not go as planned.

Use the reality of your circumstances to help you find an alternative course of action. Do it now. Don't sit around waiting for circumstances that will not change to change.

> Don't sit around waiting for circumstances that will not change to change. Patience has no effect on things that are not affected by time.

Patience has no effect on something that is not affected by time. Instead, spend time adjusting how you respond to the circumstances. It might require a changed mindset, a different plan, and a new direction. Whatever it is, take some action now, not tomorrow.

Dealing with Internal Factors

Taking action brings to the fore the internal processes necessary to deal with external factors that could impact your forward movement. It takes a response from within to deal with things that are without.

It is also important to remember that sometimes the factors that cause you to be stuck are internal and need to be addressed to get moving. On the whole, whether the primary inhibitory factors are external or internal, your internal state always plays a role. You must, therefore, deal with things within yourself as you seek to get the ball rolling.

Taking Deliberate Action

As I write this section, I am dealing with the matter of taking deliberate action to move forward. Several things have stood in the way of me completing this book. The requirements of an excessively demanding full-time job, parenting children experiencing significant challenges, including dealing with a disability, and engaging in church-related activities, among other things, leave little time to get anything else done. Getting the writing done has been quite difficult.

I, however, know that this is one thing that I need to do to move forward as I seek to fulfil that inner passion and drive. Not completing this book and others to follow would leave an irreparable void. I needed to find dedicated time to write. This included taking vacation leave to do so.

Requesting and obtaining approval for vacation leave was one step, one of many deliberate actions that I needed to take to move forward. I had some other decisions to make and actions to take to ensure that I used the moments of the few weeks I had wisely. I needed to leave my usual environment to spend time relaxing and writing.

I booked a ticket to one of my favorite getaway spots. I soon realized, however, that other things had to be considered to ensure I got the writing done. One simple yet significant thing was deciding whether to buy Malcolm Gladwell's latest book or another book to read while in flight and at other times during the vacation. I decided against doing so.

This vacation, while it was to be relaxing, was about *writing* a book, not *reading* a book. I needed to use flight time and any other significant time available to focus on thinking and writing the book. Otherwise, I could get caught up reading and spend little time writing.

To get the book done, I had to be deliberate about engaging in activities that would move that desire forward. While reading is a good thing, it was not the right action for the moments of a vacation dedicated to writing. There is a time and place for everything.

It is important to do the *right* thing in the moment. A good thing might not be the right thing. Ask yourself, "Am I doing the right thing in this moment?"

Once you have decided about the areas in which you want to move forward, it is always the right time to engage in activities that will lead to advancement in the respective areas.

As indicated earlier, self-evaluation is important, and so is planning to take deliberate action. Spend time doing specific things to move forward and try as best as possible to stick to the timelines without excuses. Use every moment wisely.

Indeed, unexpected and unavoidable things like having to take a sick child to the doctor will crop up. However, don't extend the time to deal with other things beyond when you need to. Get back to substantial activity as soon as you can. Don't delay.

One can take some pointers from James Clear on this. In the book *Atomic Habits,* he gives guidance on how to build good habits and break bad ones. He recommends consistently doing things that foster positive habits essential for growth and helping one to get better each day. He says: "Don't break the chain."

James Clear also acknowledges that lapses are inevitable as life will interrupt at times. He suggests a rule for dealing with such situations: "Never miss twice." This is a recipe for recovering quickly from interruptions and getting back to activities that will move you forward as quickly as possible. Perfection is not possible, but avoiding multiple lapses is.

Get back to doing what you need to be doing as quickly as possible, even if you cannot do it perfectly. Keep showing up for yourself. James Clear says, "The first mistake is never the one that ruins you. It is the spiral of repeated mistakes that follows. Missing once is an accident. Missing twice is the start of a new habit."[23]

There are indeed things that do impact the carrying out of desired actions; however, to what extent do such intervening variables justify not doing other essential things? Could you give too much power to intervening factors when further thought and deliberative action could result in alternative, more beneficial actions?

Said another way, when you consider the reasons for not moving forward now, is the benefit derived from whatever else is being done worth more than what would be achieved otherwise? In other words, is the action being taken to deal with some intervening factor moving you forward in some other way? It is important to do a cost-benefit analysis of the possible options.

> *The first mistake is never the one that ruins you. It is the spiral of repeated mistakes that follows. Missing once is an accident. Missing twice is the start of a new habit.*
> —James Clear

[23] Clear, J. (2018). *Atomic Habits: An easy proven way to build good habits and break bad ones.* New York: Avery. (page 201).

What is it costing to do or not to do something, and what are the rewards? In what way is the immediate action leading to your advancement? If you are truly desirous of going forward, whatever takes you away from your plan to move forward in one area should be advantageous in some other dimension of your life. If it does not add to your life, it wastes your time.

To give yourself the greatest possibility for success, moving you forward, make a plan and stick to the plan as best as possible. Don't make excuses, and avoid distractions.

Avoiding Excuses

Let's talk a little about making excuses. To make an excuse is to offer justification or reason for a behaviour, in this case, not engaging in some activity that will move you forward. Excuses can take many forms.

You can be in denial, suggesting that something does not exist or is not what it really is. You can also distort information that makes things appear better or worse than they really are, and so continue to engage in actions that are less than helpful or not engage in activities that would be more helpful.

For example, not being successful in an application to attend a desired school or obtain a scholarship does not mean that you are not smart enough and, therefore, cannot be successful academically. To say that, "I am not bright enough" or "I am not meant to pursue" academics would be a distortion of information. Lack of success in one area does not translate into not being able to achieve success in some other area, even if they are in some way related. To not put out sufficient effort to understand and do well in academic subjects or to not pursue academic subjects because of such reasoning would be an excuse.

It is important to note that excuses come from the individual who should perform the required action—the person who should be moving forward. The excuse represents something that the person tells him or herself that prevents him or her from doing what is to be done.

Excuses stem from cognitive distortions, which are thoughts that cause individuals to perceive reality inaccurately and usually involve negative thinking patterns.

Distorted thinking, which gives way to excuses, include:

- *labeling* (classifying oneself negatively after the occurrence of an adverse event).
- *mental filtering* (focusing on negative information and devaluing positive information).
- *overgeneralization* (assuming that the occurrence of one negative event means that additional bad things will happen).
- *mindreading* (assuming that others are thinking negatively about oneself).
- *catastrophizing* (making negative predictions about the future based on little or no evidence).
- *all-or-nothing thinking* (viewing something as either-or, without considering the full spectrum and range of possible evaluations).

- *emotional reasoning* (believing something to be true based on emotional responses rather than objective evidence).

- *personalization* (assuming that one is the cause of a negative event).

- *should statements* (thinking that things must or should be a certain way).

- *minimizing* (ignoring or dismissing positive things that have happened).[24]

Upon reflection, which of these ten thinking errors might you have used, albeit unwittingly, to justify the reason for not taking some necessary action? Which of these distorted cognitions represent the way you have thought about your experiences?

For example, if you are thinking, "My life is too complicated at the moment to address that now," it suggests some mental filtering. That is, you are focusing so much on the negative experiences that you fail to see the positive aspects of your life that can be put to good use in the meantime.

Similarly, saying things like, "I don't know the right people," "X said it wouldn't work, so I am not going to attempt it," and "I've got too many urgent things to do" can usually be connected with some distorted thinking, providing

---

[24] Rnic, K, Dozois, D.J.A, & Martin, R. A. (2016). *Cognitive distortions, humor styles, and depression.* Eur J Psychol, 12 (3) 348 -362. Retrieved from https://www.ncbi.nlm.nih.gov/pmc/articles/PMC4991044/

---

unjustified reasons for not taking important action to move forward. These are ultimately excuses.

Look at your reasons for not advancing in some aspect of your life. If you have not formally offered a reason but are experiencing some paralysis, an underlying reason has prevented you from taking the necessary action. Look within yourself to identify this. Are you telling yourself the truth about the situation? You might need to do some reframing as you look at the situation and associated thoughts and feelings from another angle.

To reframe the situation, you will need to rethink as you question your thoughts. Yes, think about what you are thinking about. Mind your mind. Identify where there are cognitive distortions and the underlying assumptions. Challenge the unhealthy thoughts as you unpack the assumptions. After challenging the assumptions, identify options for action in keeping with the revised thinking about the situation.

Take the necessary steps to carry out the selected action as soon as possible. Remain in the driver's seat of your life through conscious, healthy thoughts that lead to deliberate positive actions. Do not relegate the driving in your life to your unconscious mind driven by faulty assumptions. Live in the place of truth.

Dealing with Distractions

There is always something else to do, something else that seems interesting. However, that other thing is a distraction once it keeps you from concentrating on what you should be doing to advance. Distractions keep you from using available moments wisely.

Oh, how often we find so many other things to do besides what we really ought to be doing. Watching one video clip, which should last approximately three minutes, quickly turns into hours after giving in to the urge to watch just one more. Doing *just* one more is not one. In a sense, you could suppose that the activity would be carried out one additional time before turning to another activity, which would appear to be reasonable. The word *just* is misleading.

The word *just* in the statement does not give any limit, boundary or reasonable context that can be used to judge when something is achieved. In fact, it opens up the possibility for an arbitrary number or amount of something. The Urban dictionary thus gives the meaning of *just one more* as many more of something as it takes for you to achieve a satisfactory result. Therefore, if after the first video clip, your desire for laughter is further evoked and not satisfied by the first clip, you will reach out for another and another until the desire is satiated once the supply remains available.

We often fool ourselves into believing that saying something will be done just one more time means it will be done only once, and then we would return to the real task at hand. In this way, things that distract us from the real adventure take more of our time, attention, and other resources than we had imagined or intended. To avoid the trap, it is important to be aware of this fallacy and remain alert to

> *Motivation gets you going, but discipline keeps you growing.*
> *—John Maxwell*

anything that might unwittingly keep you from accomplishing more important tasks.

One way to get going with important tasks is to set limits. As with properties, boundaries serve as a demarcation for how far one is allowed to operate. It is similarly useful to set limits on how much time is to be spent doing an activity, how long something should be, how often something should be done, what order things should be done in, and so on.

Working within such boundaries should ensure that what needs to get done should get done. To ensure that the limits set provide useful guides for the accomplishment of goals, consideration should be given to allotting more time and higher priority to things of greater importance.

Setting limits is one thing; however, working within the boundaries is another. It requires discipline to stick to the plan, to take only the fifteen minutes set aside for a break to watch that video clip and not search for the full movie that could last up to five or more hours. It takes more than the motivation that got one to set the limits in the first place to keep one consistently following the set limits.

In *The 15 Invaluable Laws of Growth*, John Maxwell says: "Motivation gets you going, but discipline keeps you growing." He calls this the law of consistency. He found understanding the reason to do something was not enough to get people to actually do the right thing and to keep doing the right thing. To grow, people need to master themselves. They need to direct their determination to do things they might not like to do and consistently repeat small disciplines.

Recently, I happened upon a thought that says one should rely on discipline, not motivation. This is in keeping with John Maxwell's law of consistency. It will take more than motivation if you are to really advance.

Motivation says, "I want to, I am interested, I believe this is something to be done, and it is something I am going to work at." Motivation, however, will not get the thing done. It is the discipline to take the necessary steps and pursue the necessary actions that will result in the thing being done. We are at the point where discipline is required. It is necessary but not sufficient to have good ideas and plans. We should not soon forget the adage that the road to hell is paved with good intentions.

If you are like many, you might have been motivated for quite some time to exercise but have still not been getting it done. I was motivated to write for a long time but did not get it done until I disciplined myself to do what was necessary to complete a book. After you know what to do, you have to discipline yourself to take the steps, one at a time, to get done what needs to be done. Keep repeating the steps over time, and it will become a habit. The things you consistently do become habits.

The journey to growth, to advancement, to going forward can begin right now once the decision is made to start doing so. It happens when you change something done daily in keeping with where you want to go. What needs doing or what needs undoing to begin your forward motion? Start doing so today. Commit to acting in a similar way daily and do so regardless of the obstacles.

Yes, you must be conscious that obstacles will present themselves. You must be willing to do and be in spite of the obstacles. That is the discipline that will create the habits that will see you advancing as you overcome distractions to achieve the goal. Don't give in to distractions.

Overcoming Procrastination

Before I end this chapter, I would like to address the issue of procrastination briefly. This is another challenge some individuals have that can keep them from going forward sooner. As I think about this concept, a memory gem that I learned when I was a child comes to mind. It says, "Procrastination is the thief of time."

Indeed, postponing things unnecessarily causes a lot of time to be wasted. Taking action in a timely manner instead of delaying is thus advised. A wise person would do well to put into practice anything that has been learned as soon as possible. For many, this is easier said than done. They delay in dealing with matters in one or more spheres of their lives, which inevitably has negative implications. Overcoming procrastination will involve first realizing that one is doing it, recognizing what is causing it, and then finding the right strategy to manage and overcome it.

Procrastination involves avoiding urgent tasks that should be a priority and instead focusing on less important, more enjoyable, or simpler tasks. Some causes of procrastination include lack of motivation, low self-confidence, low self-esteem, fear of failure, fear of criticism, lack of understanding, trouble concentrating, perfectionism, low energy levels, poor organizational skills, inability to manage moods around a task, decision fatigue, and avoidance.

Some ways to overcome procrastination include:

1. Breaking down large tasks into smaller manageable parts so that the task can be tackled step by step and does not look so overwhelming or daunting. Approach the activity one step at a time—one thing at a time. Each small win will eventually lead to an overall victory.

2. Ensuring that you are moving forward in a meaningful and relevant area for you. It will be harder to get started on something that does not have your true interest and that you are not truly connected to. You will likely not have much motivation for something you have little interest in or are connected to.

3. Getting involved in confidence-building activities. This might be necessary if you find that you are procrastinating because you are afraid to fail or think you cannot live up to expectations. It is useful to boost your confidence as you consider your past achievements and the skills and competencies you possess that can lead to success.

4. Take care of your body by eating healthy, getting lots of sleep, and dealing with known medical conditions.

A body that is functioning well will have the energy required to get tasks done.

5. Setting clear and realistic goals and managing expectations can help one deal with the fear of failure and perfectionism that sometimes lead to procrastination. Work towards reasonable, manageable goals as you track your progress. Also, accept that it is okay to fail.

6. Accepting that it is also okay to get going on a project or task before everything is in place as long as all the necessary elements for the aspect of the task to be done are available. Acquiring the required resources to undertake the venture is part of the movement necessary to reach the goal. Unfortunately, sometimes people get so caught up in desiring the outcome and forget about the process to arrive at the outcome. Begin with what you have now.

7. Focusing on getting unpleasant tasks out of the way quickly and tackling the hardest tasks at your peak when you are most productive.

8. Getting help to address medical and mental health concerns that affect one's mood that, in turn, makes it hard to get things done. Depression is a primary factor in this context. It is important to address issues of stress, anxiety, low self-esteem, and self-blame.

Focus on what matters and make what matters your priority. If advancing matters to you, it should be at the centre of your focus while you keep the following in mind:

- Don't tolerate excuses from yourself.
- Set targets and work towards them.
- Hold yourself accountable.
- Overcome procrastination.

Start or continue moving forward today. Don't waste another moment of your life.

Reflections and Notes

How have your perspectives been transformed based on the concepts that were highlighted in this chapter? What external or internal factors are preventing you from moving forward now, and how might you deal with them?

_____

_____

_____

_____

_____

_____

_____

_____

WHEN DO I GO FORWARD?

_____

_____

_____

_____

_____

_____

_____

_____

_____

_____

_____

_____

_____

_____

_____

_____

_____

_____

_____

_____

_____

_____

_____

_____

CHAPTER 8

WHEN WILL I KNOW I HAVE MOVED FORWARD ENOUGH?

Congratulations! So, you have started to take the steps to move forward. It might be an action taken, a decision made, a perspective change, or something else. Whatever it is, you have done something that puts you in a better place than you were before psychologically, emotionally, financially, spiritually, in your health, relationship, or some other aspect of your life.

Having come some distance, gotten some results, seen some change, other questions loom: How far forward is far enough? Can I stop here? Is there a point when I should stop? When is it okay to stop? As I consider these questions, I reflect on some persons who have continued to make their mark well into their senior years.

I was pleased to be leading a service in which a 90-year-old mother in my church was celebrated in 2022. She has continued to be an example for the believers through her prayerful contributions and faithful attendance at church services, including fasting services on Wednesdays, where she continues to play a leading role. Mother Ivy Brooks' gait might have slowed, but she has continued to move forward in the work of Christian service and ministry.

I also think about my own mother, who took her role as a minister's wife seriously and thus served alongside my father faithfully until his death. One would have thought that after his passing and entering the 9th decade of life, she would think it was time to slow down or take things easier with respect to church ministry. She, however, now asks, "What else can I do? How can I continue to be engaged in the work of the church?" She seeks to participate in church services as often as possible, both in-person and virtually, always offering to be a companion on ministry trips—a true evangelist. The ministry of "helps" is her true passion. She is always thinking about others, finding ways to help and give to those in need. For her, like my dad, serving will continue to be a way of life until death or when she is no longer physically able to do so.

Another person for whom death is the ultimate marker for moving forward is my mentor, John Maxwell. At 76 years old, he continues to be deliberate about his personal growth, making time every day to read, think, file, ask questions, and write. He has already written more than 100 books, including workbooks, and is in the process of writing and teaching principles from other books yet to be published, with more in the pipeline. I was blessed to be at a Live2Lead session where he taught on principles of high-road leadership from a book he is writing. For John Maxwell, there is no finish line. He believes that you do not need a finish line if you keep growing, learning, or gaining. "When you cross a self-imposed finish line, you are done," he says.

Persons like John Maxwell, my parents, and Mother Brooks will know that they have moved forward enough in their life of service and significance when they have drawn their last breath. That is when there is nothing else that they can physically do in the present life as we know it. Death will become their ultimate finish line. I also believe that is true for many other persons. If this is not true for you, it is worth rethinking the self-imposed finish line that you might have drawn. Don't stop living before your life is done.

However, before you get to the finish line, there might be aspects of life you cannot or should not move forward with. There are things that were useful at one time that might not serve such a purpose at another time. There are activities you should discontinue and things you must give up as you move forward. It is important to know when to stop doing some things and when to commence others.

Revising or Discontinuing Activities

The truth is, nothing in this life lasts forever. As good as something is, there comes a time when it might no longer be fit for purpose and, therefore, needs to be revised, changed, or discontinued. It is important to know when any of these states have been reached for the appropriate action to be taken in order to keep going forward.

In an earlier chapter, I shared the story of my aborted trip to the Blue Mountain Peak. I have every intention of making that journey in the near future. It is a feat yet to be accomplished. Amidst everything else that I would have accomplished, I would not have moved forward far enough if there was something that I desired to do that was attainable with available resources but which I have not done.

I anxiously look forward to attaining the goal of reaching the Blue Mountain peak in the near future. I am putting plans in place to this end. I anticipate the experience, the scenery, and the picturesque moments. I will take in the beauty of the landform and its surroundings for as long as I can. I know, however, that there will be a point when I will have had my fill and will need to leave the Blue Mountain peak to return to my normal duties and explore other adventures. While reaching the Blue Mountain peak will be momentous, living there is not an option.

> *Treat each positive experience as one of many that you will have throughout life—not one of one or one of a few.*

Having reached the peak and done what I set out to accomplish, there will be no point remaining longer than necessary. After I have spent enough time savoring the experience, it will be time to stop that encounter, turn around, and head home.

Staying longer than necessary will not extend the meaning or things to be gained and could, in fact, be dangerous. In this case, the activity needs to be discontinued. It is important to note when something has reached the point when it no longer serves a useful purpose. It was good while it lasted, but it will not last forever.

Too often, I have seen persons try to remain in or return to a state where they once had some great experience, not realizing that it was not meant to be a permanent state. You should enjoy and make the most of the experience while it lasts, but be prepared to move on. Treat each positive experience as one of many that you will have throughout life— not one of one or one of a few.

The thought that, "This is good, so let me stay here since I cannot guarantee that I will find anything like this again," is a limiting mindset. Know that there are many opportunities to have positive experiences besides the ones that you have already encountered. Actively seek after those other experiences. Don't build a house where you should pitch a tent.

Evaluation is necessary to determine how to treat experiences. Yes, even positive experiences should be evaluated. This is important to determine if the place where you have arrived is somewhere to remain and continue to build. Is it a place with an encounter that you could seek to replicate, maybe at the same place or elsewhere at other times, or is it a place with a one-off encounter where the memories will suffice? All of these represent different ways of moving forward with regard to a positive experience.

Things that are essential to life and livelihood might require setting down some roots. Thus, things that address basic or primary needs related to food, clothing, shelter, education, transportation, and health will require making some long-term decisions to affect things for an extended period. In such cases, setting down roots in some things would be helpful, like purchasing that house in a community that you recently drove through, liked, and can afford. Buying that car that you saw in the showroom to make it easier to reach work on time and take the children to school and other activities might also be a worthwhile venture.

Continuing experiences that will work to satisfy or enhance the satisfaction of basic needs are advised. Further evaluation should be done for experiences that are related to secondary or tertiary needs. Secondary needs can be seen as those desires and wants associated with pleasure and satisfaction beyond the fulfilment of primary needs. These include the need for safety and security, achievement, esteem, affection, power, and belonging. Secondary needs are complementary to primary needs in order to live a better quality of life. For example, it is important to have somewhere to live—a primary need; however, where you live and the furnishings in the house would represent a secondary need.

Tertiary needs are third in the level of priority and are a complement to personal pleasure. Humans can continue their lives if tertiary needs are not fulfilled. A vacation abroad or purchasing some luxury item would be a tertiary need. My life has continued, although I have not yet made it to the Blue Mountain peak—a tertiary need.

Where an experience caters to a secondary or tertiary need, if its continuation will lead to further growth and continued enhanced quality of life, then it is worth exploring for an extended duration. If there is nothing to be gained beyond the basic pleasure and lessons from the experience, then once those are exhausted, it is worth ending that experience. Life should not be lived as an extended vacation. Treasure the memories and move on. Prolonging such experience will eventually lead to negative returns.

There are other times when you are going forward when things need to be revised or changed. In such situations, you would have gone forward far enough in a particular mode, and a revision would need to be done. Continuing in the same mode would not be the most effective way to operate. This situation was evident when the COVID-19 pandemic struck.

There were schools and businesses that were operating effectively prior to the COVID-19 pandemic. Others were not as effective but were taking steps toward improvement. They were going forward. The nature of the pandemic meant that persons needed to be distanced to avoid contact that could result in the spread of the coronavirus. This had implications for many operations which were built around physical interaction between people. To continue to survive and operate during the pandemic meant that things needed to change.

> *Life should not be lived as an extended vacation. Treasure the memories and move on.*

Ways had to be found to continue to interact at some distance. This need saw the introduction of social distancing (physical distancing) rules, which required persons to remain about six feet from each other in offices and other gathering places. Persons were required to wear masks. Vaccination and COVID-19 testing were, at points, required for international travel. Schools and businesses initiated work-from-home protocols and were compelled to make use of online technology for teaching and learning and to conduct business.

Persons who were able to make the adjustment fared much better than those who were not able to do so. As a result, a number of businesses closed, and students who were not able to access lessons have fallen behind academically.

Things do not have to be as monumental as the COVID-19 pandemic, which has affected the entire world. In our daily lives, things happen that require us to take stock and make necessary adjustments. To this end, you are encouraged to be reflective (analyze what has happened) and reflexive (self-adjust and respond to the circumstances as they are happening) and make these regular habits. Reflection and reflexivity involve thinking about and examining your feelings, reactions,

> *Too often people try to live their current lives based on past realities.*

and motives and how they influence what you do. It means questioning assumptions that you might have taken for granted.

Life is also different after the COVID-19 pandemic. What have you reflected on since, and how have you readjusted to life in the different spheres? Constant evaluation and reevaluation are necessary to determine what is working and what is not, what is effective and what is not, given the current circumstances.

Too often, people try to live their current lives based on past realities. If the way you are living does not match your current reality, it means that some adjustment needs to be made to match the circumstances. You would have gone forward far enough in that mode. A new or revised mode is needed.

For example, strictly online meetings were necessary during the height of the COVID-19 pandemic, but does this still remain the case? How might a blend of online and face-to-face meetings be utilized for maximum effect? What adjustments might I need to make in my own thinking and approach to facilitate this?

You have gone forward far enough in a mode of operation when it is no longer yielding maximum results in the circumstances in which it is being used. Some adjustment is necessary.

Reaching Goals

While reaching the mountain peak in itself is a great accomplishment, you must also determine if just getting to the peak is all that is desired. In the field of education, we refer to goals and objectives. There are also general and specific objectives for activities. The broad overall aim can be broken down into smaller outcomes. The broad aim or goal might be to reach the mountain peak, but is that all?

What do you hope to accomplish by going to the peak? If just reaching the peak is the goal and there are no other objectives, then having set foot on the highest point of the mountain, you can simply turn around and head back down. Mission accomplished! Tick it off the bucket list. You would have gone far enough.

However, while not everything should be pursued with an ulterior motive, it is prudent to garner the benefits to be had from an experience. Otherwise, time and effort would be spent doing something that might be of little real value. That time could otherwise be spent on things that are more meaningful to your life, thereby moving you further ahead. This brings to mind a point raised in an earlier chapter: moving ahead with an activity does not always move you forward. In fact, taking the time to do something that has no real value could actually be a retrograde step.

If reaching the Blue Mountain peak is to be truly meaningful, there are experiences on the peak that need to be captured and understood. Just stepping on the peak will not be good enough. Other things must be done to satisfy the other reasons for going to the peak. You will know you have gone far enough when you satisfy your inner desires that drove you to the activity.

Did you use your binoculars to try to spot Cuba? Did you take in the sunrise? Did you lay flat on your back and look up to the skies like you wanted? Did you stay long enough to meditate and have that spiritual encounter that could only be experienced in that moment, in that place? Don't be satisfied with just reaching the peak. Stretch yourself a little more using your other faculties to have experiences at the peak that will take you forward even further.

Going forward is more than just a physical journey or activity. Going forward might involve different types of movement even in the same situation. Besides moving forward physically, you can advance cognitively, emotionally, psychologically, spiritually, and in other areas.

Arriving at the mountain peak is indeed a physical accomplishment. But beyond that, it is also an extraordinary feat of endurance and triumph in itself. It is a psychological accomplishment that should not go unnoticed or be trivialized. You would shortchange yourself if only the physical aspect of the journey is considered in arriving at the peak.

Take time to acknowledge and have other life-changing encounters at the peak and on your journey to the peak. Enjoy the ride! There are significant social, emotional, spiritual, and other life-changing encounters that are possible from the experience. Be open to considering the various possibilities. Set some goals.

Setting goals and objectives will be important as you move forward. These will give focus to your activities. They will also provide a means for evaluating how far you have gone in the journey. Where goals are successfully accomplished, it is okay to celebrate that win and move on. Look towards accomplishing something else. Set another goal to move further. Keep setting and achieving goals.

> *Let the attainment of one goal become the marker for setting and reaching another goal.*

Let the attainment of one goal become the marker for setting and reaching another goal. Each goal then becomes a significant milestone to be celebrated along the journey. The journey should not end with the accomplishment of goals. Yes, pause, celebrate, and take stock. Set another goal and head in the direction of the new goal.

Respecting Boundaries

In determining whether you have gone far enough, understanding boundaries is important. These represent parameters set to determine the limits of how far you can reasonably go. When night falls, there are some things that are not feasible. Going too near to the edge of the mountain without sufficient lighting could result in a fall if you are not able to discern your steps.

Whatever you do, it is important to pay attention to reasonable limits and boundaries and use them as guiding posts to know when you have done enough. You can suffer consequences for going beyond reasonable boundaries.

One example of this relates to the care of the body. Yes, push as far as you can to get as much done as you can. There, however, comes a point when lack of sleep cannot be sustained, and you will have to stop going and get some rest. There are times when rest is required along the journey. Know when you have come upon a boundary, when you have reached your limit, and stop.

The terms *burnout* and *fatigue* are worth knowing. They can affect even people doing very good things. Yes, you can become tired, overwhelmed, stressed, and frustrated from doing things that are useful in moving you forward if proper precautions are not taken to avoid stretching beyond your capacity.

So far, the concern has been with reasonable boundaries that serve as safeguards from physical or psychological harm. However, there are times when the boundaries are arbitrary and need to be revised. Your role in going forward could be to help redefine such boundaries and act within larger boundaries such as laws, ethical principles, and your guiding values.

Effects

Other considerations in determining if you have gone far enough are the effects you are experiencing. Going forward is about improving yourself, achieving more, and generally moving in a direction where life is better, and things are better. It is about advancing.

Therefore, you should evaluate yourself to determine if you are indeed continuing to experience moreness in the various aspects of life. You are encouraged to continue on the path where moreness is being experienced.

A question that you might ask is, "To what extent am I experiencing peace on this journey?" A place of peace is to be desired. The Scriptures encourage one to seek after peace and pursue it (see Psalm 34:14). If you have found peace on the forward path, it would be good to determine what in the process has resulted in the peace being experienced. That should be continued, or more should be done to experience even greater peace.

Other questions that can be asked are, "How is my health? Am I experiencing greater health and well-being as I go forward?" It is a good sign if you are doing better and feeling better. It suggests that you are moving in the right direction. You are going forward. You should, however, not get complacent and be satisfied with the movement that has begun. You should continue on the path that will lead to further changes until you are at your best in health and well-being. When that level is achieved, it should be maintained.

Too often, people stop doing the things that are having a positive effect at early signs of good results. This is often not deliberate but unwitting. People too soon begin to take some things for granted. Consistency and persistency are required to experience continued positive results. Work will continue to be necessary to experience positive results. Going forward is a continual process that can last a lifetime.

> *Too often, people stop doing the things that are having a positive effect at early signs of good results. Consistency and persistency are required to experience continued positive results.*

What do you need to start doing again to return to a state of health in your relationships and other aspects of your life? What might you have been taking for granted after a while because it was working well initially? Going forward will require constant work. There are some aspects of going forward that should not be stopped or paused.

Another question that could be asked is, "How have I grown?" If you are growing as you are going, then that is a good state to be in. Since one is dying if one is not growing, growth is a desirable state. Continue to engage with the things on the journey that are leading to your growth, and keep away from those things that have the potential to stop your growth. Keep moving in the direction in which you are growing.

We can conclude that there is no true reason to stop going forward if you are learning, growing, advancing, experiencing peace, or a general sense of moreness in your endeavors. It is important to pay attention to goals, boundaries, and other effects to determine when to pause, stop, or change some things to keep going forward.

Reflections and Notes

How have your perspectives been transformed based on the concepts that were highlighted in this chapter? What markers will you use to determine how far forward you have moved and should continue to move in the various aspects of your life: social, spiritual, emotional, physical, financial, etc.?

_____

_____

_____

_____

_____

_____

_____

_____

_____

_____

_____

_____

_____

_____

WHY?

CHAPTER 9

WHY SHOULD I MOVE FORWARD?

I am alive, breathing, existing, and taking each day as it comes, so what's the big deal about going forward? Isn't being alive good enough? The quick response is, "It is not enough just to be breathing." One can be breathing and not truly alive.

Someone else might say I have already achieved much success and am doing productive things, so this going forward thing is not really about me. Have you maximized your potential in every area of your life or done all that you can with what you have? If that response is a no, then going forward is also for you

Let us look further into the reasons to go forward.

Desiring More

I teach a professional development course for in-service educators. Very often, participants question the necessity of such a course, especially since they are already working in the education system. I would normally ask, "In your present teaching career, in whatever subject area you teach, are all your students passing with the maximum marks possible in all your classes?" The resounding response is always "No."

My follow-up is usually this: "Until all your students are getting the maximum possible marks in all your classes all the time, there is room for improvement, and there is something you can change to help facilitate that."

About this time, hands are raised to respond quickly to this statement. One of the responses is usually, "Everyone is always blaming teachers for everything; the students and parents are not doing what they should do, and nobody is talking to them about that."

I smile when I get such feedback as I have a retort. "Indeed so! That's where you come in. You are one of the persons who interact with parents and students. You need to learn how to communicate more effectively with them so they can understand and better play their role in the learning process. Teaching is about facilitating learning, and facilitating learning is more than delivering content."

With that statement, I know I have preached a sermon and dropped a bombshell. Participants quickly recognize that more growth is necessary on their part. Firstly, there are assumptions that many have about the nature of their roles that need to be addressed. Then, there are skills and competencies to be acquired for greater effectiveness in the role. Is there a need for professional development? Yes.

Teachers of two years or twenty have room for improvement. Those who accept this state of affairs and ultimately desire to contribute to improved educational outcomes will strive to develop or improve themselves so that their roles as teachers are positively impacted. Such teachers have found a reason to go forward.

I will ask you some questions similar to the ones I ask my students. Look at the various roles that you play in life, paid or unpaid. For each of the roles, evaluate the successes and failures. Are all the people you are connected to in this role experiencing maximum results or benefits? Are they the best that they can be? Consider the ratio of people who have been leaving the organization or team. Is it acceptable? If the role is more

> *You cannot remain at the same place that you are to go where you are going.*

task-based, are all the activities completed in the best possible way, leading to the best possible effect or results? When you consider other markers of true success and effectiveness, are they all resoundingly positive? If the answer to any of these is no, there is room for improvement to maximize results in that sphere. There is more that can be accomplished, and that is a reason to go forward.

We will not lose sight of the personal relationship. Yes, that relationship you have with yourself. Are you doing all the things you can in all the ways you can to get the best possible results? Are you satisfied with the results and experiences in every area of your life? If the answer to these is no, that is another reason to go forward. There is something else to be achieved, something more to be accomplished. If you remain satisfied with where you are and what you are doing, then there will be no impetus to do anything differently to get more.

From the references so far, we realize that going forward is the way to access more, achieve more, be more, do more in our personal and professional lives. A crucial question must therefore be answered in determining the reason to go forward. The question is, "Do you desire something more?" If there is ever a desire for more, for something better in any aspect of your life, then something will need to be done to advance in the desired area. That is a reason to go forward. Yes, that is why you should go forward.

If you desire it, go for it. There are few people who will get more based on sheer luck. An old grand-aunt leaving her wealth to you is more likely to happen in the movies than in real life. Most people acquire wealth through their own deliberate efforts from their work and investments. This is also true for other things to be achieved in life. Personal effort is usually necessary to get something more. You need to desire it and take the necessary action to achieve it. Reach for it. Go forward.

In what aspect of your life do you desire more? Yes, believe to see it manifested. Exercise your faith. However, as the Bible teaches, faith without works is dead (see James 2:26). One must act in the area where faith is being exercised to see the results. That action in agreement with your faith is the way to go forward.

It is important to avoid falling into the trap of stagnation. This is a state marked by a lack of movement. It is as if life comes to a standstill. One can be running on the treadmill of life, engaging in mundane daily activities but not really moving forward. A lack of movement suggests a lack of growth. Growth is evidence of life. Lack of movement in an area could, in effect, mean that you are, in fact, dying in that area. Don't die before your death. Desire more. Keep going forward.

Besides desiring more and avoiding stagnation, what other reasons are there to move forward? There are other realities of life that warrant actions that will move us forward. These include responding to changes and challenges.

Dealing with Change

Some years ago, I was introduced to the book *Who Moved My Cheese?* by Spencer Johnson. The allegory involves four characters who live in a maze in which they are looking for things they desire to have, represented in the story as Cheese.

They eventually each found their favorite Cheese. How did it come to be there, where did it come from, or who had put it there? They did not know. They had found what they wanted and just assumed it would be there. Something, however, happened one morning when the characters arrived at the cheese station. There was no Cheese. This was not a surprise for two of the characters who were more animal-like. Upon realizing the inevitable, they went elsewhere to find new Cheese.

The other characters, who were more human-like, were unprepared for what they found. They were not ready for this. They ranted and raved about the situation, which they considered an injustice done to them. But the Cheese never reappeared.

Eventually, one of the two human-like characters realized that the longer they stayed in the Cheese-less situation, the worse off they were becoming. He decided to push past the fears that kept him in the maze and learned to adapt. He set out to find new Cheese, learning lessons along the way. He tried to persuade his friend to do the same but was unable to sway him. His friend remained in denial and continued to resist change as he believed it would lead to something worse. He never found new Cheese.

Spencer Johnson's tale on change bears much resemblance to real life. We often say change is the only constant, meaning that change is inevitable. While this might be true, we are often unprepared for some changes and do not readily adapt to deal with them. There are some aspects in our lives where we readily accept changes, while there are others that we are less willing to accept and deal with.

Stagnant water is an environmental and health hazard. Similarly, stagnation is a hazard to one's health and well-being.

For example, it is expected that a child will grow in height and will also gain weight. As such, things are usually put in place to provide the clothes to fit, and larger meals are prepared to meet the nutritional demands of the growing child. It is also anticipated that as one grows older, one's educational level will change. The fees that will be required to complete higher levels of education will be higher. It is, therefore, acceptable to use savings or take out loans to finance higher education.

I observe with interest a number of situations where a similar expectation of change and preparation for same is not made in adult life, such as in relationships. People enter relationships with their partners having a certain physique. Over time, however, the daily responsibilities, life tasks, and the natural aging process lead to changes in one's physical features. The woman who gave birth might have stretch marks and breasts that sag. A more sedentary man who continues to eat the same amount as when he was younger might have a larger stomach than in his younger years.

Instead of acknowledging these changes as natural and adjusting expectations and actions accordingly, some relationships end up being destroyed as a result. People divorce or leave their partners because someone else looks better physically and catches their fancy. Some remain in the relationship physically but exist in a continuous state of dissatisfaction.

What makes it easier to accept the physical changes in a younger person but not older persons undergoing the same natural aging process? What causes us to accept that as one gets older, knowledge should increase and changes in educational level are expected for younger persons; however, after leaving school and finding a job, we expect to stay in the same job forever or at least for quite a long time? What causes us to expect that something that worked at one time in one situation will work all the time in all contexts when the variables have changed? If change is inevitable, why do we expect some things to change and not others? What is it that puts some things out of the realm of what can be changed or what we can expect to change? In this regard, we should consciously reflect on our thoughts and attitudes toward change.

There are some realities related to change that you need to deal with in order to move forward. Not doing so will lead to much distress as there are some things you will lose and might never regain, and which could be detrimental to your overall well-being. By the same token, there are some new things that need to be embraced in order to move forward. Sticking slavishly to things that have outgrown their purpose, usefulness, or effectiveness can be more destructive than they are helpful.

You should be cautious to examine your life and that of groups and institutions over which you have some control to see if there is any area where you have been reluctant or unwilling to change. What has been the result of such a stance? Yes, the real effect, the true results, not only the aspects that look good. How have you been feeling? How is your health? What have been the complaints? How many persons have been hurt? What is the attrition rate? What have persons been trying to say to you that you have gotten angry with them about and avoid dealing with because you do not want to change?

Some people's lives are stuck in a rut, institutions are in a mess, relationships are being destroyed, and many unhealthy situations exist because there are changes that need to be made; however, this is not happening. No one is willing to bell the cat. Change is necessary if they are ever going to reach an optimal state. Things will only become better if they move forward—if they make positive changes. Remaining as they are will lead to a worse state.

By nature, there are some persons who adapt to change less readily, such as people with a high S on the DISC personality profile. It is important to know when changes are necessary and be flexible enough to adapt, even if it means getting help.

If you don't change when you ought to, you run the risk of dying an early death or experiencing other unfavourable outcomes. Stagnation could result from not changing. Water that does not flow—is not changing—is stagnant and is a breeding ground for bacteria and insects like mosquitoes that transmit diseases. Stagnant water is an environmental hazard. Similarly, stagnation is a hazard to your well-being. It is an unhealthy state.

Things that are not changed over time could eventually become obsolete. If people and things do not adapt to the evolving context, they could become irrelevant. Things that are irrelevant eventually find little to no use and are put away. What do you think should have had more impact but is instead being put away or ignored by others? What changes might have been made that would have made it more relevant or impactful? Changes

> *If you don't change when you ought to, you run the risk of dying an early death or experiencing other unfavourable outcomes.*

are necessary for some things to move forward.

Unfortunately, some people have become lazy. Changing requires an effort that some are not willing to expend. They would rather continue to live with something that has the appearance of working. They opt for the easy route. It looks good on the outside, although not truly effective.

Honesty with yourself will require change. If you are honest with yourself about the state of your life and institutions, you will be willing to embrace change so that you can move forward. Too many people are comfortable with settling and living a lie. Don't be one of those people.

A final thought on the matter of change. Going forward can only occur when change of some sort is involved. If one is using the feet, one foot replaces the other as one takes step after step. One foot is changed for the other. The motion of the foot includes change in angles as the foot is lifted and returned to the ground. Similarly, the wheel of a chair in motion involves changes. The rotation of the wheel means that each point of the wheel is at a different place throughout the 360-degree cycle.

The process of going forward also means that one is changing location as one moves from one place to the next, no matter how small the move. In a more symbolic way, change is necessary. You cannot remain at the same place that you are to go where you are going. To go somewhere, some change has to be involved. Change is necessary to go forward.

Dealing with Challenges

In 2020, the world faced a challenge of enormous proportions when the COVID-19 pandemic struck. As of December 29, 2022, the outbreak was said to have claimed approximately 6,691,567 lives worldwide. While life is more or less back to normal, one cannot help but reflect on this life-changing phenomenon.

According to the World Health Organization (WHO), the Coronavirus (COVID-19) is an infectious disease caused by the SARS-CoV-2 virus. It is a virus that primarily affects the respiratory system. Most persons infected with the disease were expected to experience mild to moderate symptoms, with few persons becoming seriously ill or dying.

The virus could spread from an infected person to others via the nose or mouth via droplets when they cough, sneeze, speak, sing, or breathe. This presented a significant challenge as taking a simple breath to stay alive and engaging in normal social interaction could put one at risk of contracting the disease.

At the height of the pandemic, there were many deaths, especially among the elderly and persons with underlying conditions. Healthcare systems were stretched to capacity, and there was much panic as people tried to come to grips with the reality of the situation. Thankfully, however, the number of lives lost was much less than the 20–50 million who died in the Flu pandemic between 1918 and 1920. How did we survive the pandemic, and what has put us back on our feet? There is much to be learned from this about going forward despite challenges.

As with changes, challenges are inevitable. There is no life without challenge. Sometimes, the challenges are of the common variety, like the common cold, and, in some cases, they are of a magnitude and nature beyond your wildest imagination, like the coronavirus. Whatever the nature of the challenge, it has the potential to interrupt your life and bring you to a standstill.

You do not have to give in to challenges. You can continue to be productive and effective in spite of challenges. Finding a way to go forward ensures this. We did just that during the COVID-19 pandemic when steps were taken to deal with the situation by wearing masks, keeping away from each other through physical distancing, improved sanitization practices such as washing hands, and the expedited development of vaccines. You do not have to be overcome by challenges but can instead overcome challenges by taking steps to deal with specific concerns. This is about moving forward.

You do this by minimizing the risk of exposure to the

Be careful of sacrificing yourself on the altar of other peoples' needs and desires.

dangers by taking precautions to protect yourself and others. Where you have been exposed to the danger, you should seek help as soon as possible to get the necessary support to overcome the challenge. If the available options for dealing with the challenge are limited, find ways to develop alternatives that could lead to improved outcomes.

Finding ways to deal with challenges means moving forward. The alternative would be to not move forward, thereby leaving yourself entirely vulnerable to be ravished by the challenge. You cannot afford to give in to challenges. Going forward is the way to not be overcome by challenges. It is about being resilient.

Some challenges that you may encounter have the potential to break you. This is what has led many to commit suicide. You can, however, take the decision to move forward. In so doing, you are preserving life. Going forward then becomes a life-or-death decision. Choosing to live will mean going forward.

Loving Yourself

The Bible teaches that love is the greatest virtue and that loving yourself is an aspect of the greatest commandment (see Matthew 22:39). Loving yourself entails doing what is in your best interest while at the same time not deliberately hurting others. You should love your neighbor as yourself.

It appears that persons sometimes feel that it is not okay to love self. This can leave persons feeling guilty about making decisions that put themselves first. For whatever reason, some persons have grown to believe that the right thing to do is to sacrifice themselves on the altar of others' needs and desires. This misconception needs to be corrected. Be careful of sacrificing yourself on the altar of other peoples' needs and desires.

It is okay to love yourself. It is okay to take care of yourself. It is also okay to do what is in your best interest. This will mean taking all relevant information into account. Yes, sometimes you have to be selfish. Take care of your needs, which are your responsibility, and leave others to take care of their own, which is their responsibility.

Too often, people fall into the trap of taking responsibility for things that others should be responsible for, such as their thoughts and feelings. They sometimes act to protect the thoughts and feelings of others over which they have no control, while deliberately hurting themselves in the process. People become so overly concerned about what others think and feel and with pleasing them that they end up having a mental breakdown or other health concerns in the process. This stems from loving others more than we love ourselves. The scale needs to be rebalanced. We should love others as we love ourselves, not more than we love ourselves. Yes, you should love others as you love yourself, not more than you love yourself.

Understanding boundaries will be helpful in this regard. In their book *Boundaries*, Dr. Henry Cloud and Dr. John Townsend note that, "Any confusion of responsibility and ownership in our lives is a problem of boundaries." [25] According to Dr. Cloud, many people struggle with discovering, setting, and guarding their personal boundaries, which has led to a host of problems, including depression, anxiety, identity loss, lack of purpose, and powerlessness, among others. He also notes that abuse—physical and emotional—is probably the most destructive result of a lack of boundaries. [26]

Going forward for some will mean setting and maintaining boundaries, which will ultimately lead to greater health and well-being. Loving and caring about youself means being concerned about your personal health and well-being. It is an

---

[25] Cloud, H. & Townsend, J. (2017). *Boundaries*. Zondervan. page 25.
[26] Cloud, H. (1992). *Changes that Heal*. Zondervan.

important reason to take the necessary steps to set and maintain boundaries—go forward.

Yes, it is true that self-centeredness should be avoided. That is being exclusively or excessively concerned about yourself and doing things for your advantage or pleasure without due consideration of others. You should not be only concerned about yourself. By the same token, you *should* be concerned about yourself. You should love yourself enough to look out for yourself and be good to yourself. I matter to me. Yes, you should matter to you.

Learning to love self is something that many will need to do without feeling guilty. Is that something you might need to do for yourself? That is another reason to go forward. Not taking the step to go forward, advance, and help yourself means that you do not truly love yourself. That is not a good place to be in. It is important to make yourself a priority.

> *You should matter to you. Make yourself a priority.*

So, it has been concluded that going forward is important. There is always a reason to go forward. Not going forward means settling for less than the best. Not going forward could mean dying an early death. It could mean stagnation. It could also mean succumbing to challenges that leave you in a less-than-optimal state and not effectively dealing with changes that keep you away from your Cheese. Don't lose out on what truly matters to you because you fail to move forward. Going forward is the only option if you truly care about yourself and want to make yourself a priority.

Reflections and Notes

How have your perspectives been transformed based on the concepts that were highlighted in this chapter? What is your impetus for moving forward?

_____

_____

_____

_____

_____

_____

_____

_____

_____

_____

_____

_____

_____

_____

_____

_____

_____

CHAPTER 10

WHAT IS MY WHY AS I MOVE FORWARD?

You have made it to the final chapter, or maybe you have turned to this chapter for some direct answers. Congratulations on giving serious thought to going forward and for taking decisive action!

Yes, going forward is the thing to do because you matter to yourself.

Because you care about acting in your best interest, it is important to know what you are going forward to. You should seek to maximize your potential and work efficiently and effectively. This will happen when you know the general direction in which you should be going. It is essential to have a compass bearing to end up at the right place.

It would be sad if, at the end of the trip, you realize that you took the wrong flight and ended up in the wrong place. If you landed in Boston on the way to Cambridge, England, you would be thousands of miles away. Cambridge in Massachusetts is not the same as Cambridge in England. Yes, you would have gone forward and traveled many miles;

however, you would still be in a less-than-optimal position. Additional effort and resources will have to be found to correct the error and find your way back to where you should be.

To guard against taking missteps, there are some important things to understand and be guided by in your actions. These are wrapped up in knowing your purpose. Understanding your why—what you are about and being true to this cause.

Understanding my Purpose

As presented in earlier chapters, God, the Creator, and Scriptwriter, has an ultimate aim or purpose in mind for His creation. That purpose needs to be understood to effectively carry out the role.

As no manual has been given that outlines your purpose in specific detail, this has to be inferred from the design. Some design elements to be considered in this analysis include observing your strengths and abilities, knowing your passions, and understanding your pains and context.

Passion

In an earlier chapter, reference was made to passion. This speaks to knowing where your heart lies. Passion means something that one has a strong liking or desire for.

Knowing your passion will mean being connected with and tapping into your feelings. It will require paying attention to your emotions—recognize the things that make you feel good and others that do not. Note the things that give pleasure and others, not so much.

Things that bring delight and generally evoke positive emotions are those things that will normally capture your heart. There is a reason people are usually told to follow their heart in making decisions about relationships and other critical choices. Being able to identify those things that bring joy, peace, and happiness is crucial in knowing where your heart is. The heart remains a good guide.

What is it that matters to you? What is it that moves you? This is connected to what you like and what has your heart and is a good indication of the direction in which you should be going.

Spending time with yourself will be important to understanding what matters to you. This requires taking time to connect with yourself through introspection and processes of reflection and evaluation. This will mean taking time to think about yourself, yes, yourself. This takes us back to the idea of loving yourself.

You are important, and you should love yourself enough to make time to be with yourself. Take time each day, each week, each month, and each year to reflect on yourself. Identify what piques your interest, what has your fancy, what motivates you, and what has your heart. Use that to guide your decisions as you seek to move forward.

It is important to be sure of your *why* so that you end up in a place where you want to be. Cambridge, USA might be a great place, but it will not be right for you if you like the British education system and want to be schooled in it. Although a great institution, Harvard University cannot be substituted for Cambridge if Harvard does not have your heart. One can make do with something else, but there is no substitute for whatever has your heart. Until it is achieved, there will always be a longing consciously or subconsciously for the thing that had your heart.

Spend time with yourself to know what is important to you. Connect with yourself through reflection and introspection.

It is advised to go after your heart. Find your passion. As much as possible, live and work in the area of your passion. If you cannot do so immediately, work with what you have until you can do so. Set things in motion to align with your passion as soon as possible.

Do not settle for something good or great based on what someone else likes. No one else has *your* heart. Be careful about how you take instructions from others about moving forward. Unless they are sensitive to and are seeking to guide you in the direction of your heart, others will usually create excitement around and send you in the direction of what they like and what has their heart. It is important to know the distinction between what has someone else's heart and what has your heart.

Seek to know and live in the place of your passion, not someone else's passion. Take time to know yourself, love yourself, and be true to yourself.

Pain

You might wonder why pain would be listed under a topic about understanding your why. What does pain have to do with understanding my purpose? Shouldn't the things that I like be easy for me?

In no way am I suggesting that you should seek out hard things to do, things that are painful. No one should deliberately seek out pain or take pleasure in experiencing pain or inflicting pain on others. Masochism and sadism are to be avoided.

True to life, however, you cannot overlook the fact that pain is a natural outcome of some of our experiences. Some can be avoided. There are others over which we have little control. Pain represents something that we dislike, as it is usually associated with something that hurts or causes damage.

Your response to pain can be an important factor in determining how to move forward. Firstly, it is prudent to act in a manner that minimizes the painful experience. That should give some sense of direction as you consider all possible options and then make a suitable selection. Overcoming or effectively dealing with the painful situation will certainly push you forward.

You should love yourself enough to do everything possible to reduce the pain. Do something about the thing that is hurting you. You won't get points for being a martyr. The martyr complex marked by self-sacrifice and service to others at your own expense has its drawbacks. You should not continue to victimize yourself for the benefit of others. Take steps to shift from being a martyr to taking care of yourself.

Besides dealing with pain in your own life, the pain you have experienced can be an impetus to find ways to help others deal with a similar concern. This can be a driving force in establishing organizations or working with other groups to address challenges. In so doing, you can find meaning and purpose in pain. This could point the direction for moving forward. This could lead to a life of significance as you serve others.

In *The Power of Significance,* John Maxwell notes that our purpose is our individual way of improving the world. Certainly, helping others to navigate situations that would reduce pain and its harmful effects would contribute to a better world. Maxwell further notes that living a life of significance is about making a difference with others with whatever you have. If you desire a life of significance, finding a way to serve others based on lessons learned from your days of pain is a good *why* as you go forward.

I strongly believe in using what you have. Like the story of the little girl who did not recognize that her father was a resource that she had that formed part of her strength, sometimes people forget that experiences; good or bad, and the scars or impressions, physical or otherwise, remain with them. Yes, the scar, impressions, feelings, and thoughts are things you have. It might require introspection or deeper reflection to sometimes recognize what you really have. It might be easier to enumerate tangible things that you

> *Don't discount the challenges you have faced or any experience you have. They are nontangible assets for which use can be found.*

have personally acquired or received from others. We should, however, not forget that there are other things that are just as real, though you might not be able to touch them.

As with tangible things, nontangible things can also be used for good or bad. Lessons learned from painful experiences are one such nontangible. It is something that you have that can be put to good use to benefit yourself and others. How can you deal with the pain you might be experiencing, or how could your pain help you to serve others? Answers to these questions can help you find your why as you move forward.

Find purpose in your pain. Don't discount the challenges you have faced or any experience you have had or will have. They are nontangible assets for which use can be found. Use what you have.

Strengths/Abilities

If someone needed to get anywhere speedily and had a donkey and a horse, one would question the use of the donkey in such a situation. What would make the difference in the selection? Certainly, the capabilities of the animals. A donkey takes longer travelling at a maximum of 15mph, while a horse travels between 25-40mph on average. Some horses can travel up to 55mph. One who owns horses would do well to consider entering a derby. However, the same would not be possible for someone with donkeys as the only large mammals on his farm.

Similarly, your strengths and abilities give a good indication of what you are suited for. Keen attention should be paid to determining your areas of strength, aptitudes, and abilities.

This is more than about what you like to do. It is what you can do and do well. It is what you have the propensity to be good at.

There are times when what you can do and do well is not what you are inclined to do for various reasons. There are strengths that might not be acknowledged and hidden potential that has not been tapped into. You might have been discouraged from pursuing that option because of the perception or actions of others, challenges that intervened, fears, or unrealistic expectations, among other things.

For some people, moving forward will require identifying and acknowledging areas of strength and potentiality. These can be determined by a number of things.

Firstly, look at areas in which you have natural ability. Can you sing very well? Do you find that you grasp foreign languages very quickly and might even be outstanding in one? Are you much taller than your mates and find that you are quite agile? Can you sketch and draw very well? Do you find that you are creative in the kitchen and enjoy cooking? The natural abilities that you possess present areas for exploration for further development and possible options for work. They are related to your *why*.

What have you done over time? What skills have you acquired? What competencies have you developed? Identify the main characteristics of the jobs that you have done and the roles you have played to see what skills you have acquired. Take the time to list them if you need to.

Often, people shortchange themselves as they have a limited view of what it means to do a job or activity. They often focus only on the job title. This prevents them from seeing all the other things that they would have done in the role. Everything you have done can be useful for other things you need to do, if you take the time to understand what you have done and apply relevant aspects to the new context.

> *Do not settle for something good or great based on what someone else likes. No one else has your heart.*

In this regard, the skills and competencies acquired from previous experiences can be the basis for going forward. Use what you have.

Something else that many have is knowledge. What have you studied? What have you learned informally through your own research and experimentation? The efforts you would have placed into studying and gaining certification in an area have value and should not be discounted.

In some instances, what you have studied might not be what you originally wanted to do. This could cause you to somehow downplay what has been accomplished and, therefore, might not utilize the knowledge much. In moving forward, it is important to acknowledge what you have, although it might not be what is ultimately desired. The fact that you completed the course means that there is something about the programme that you can work with. Find what works for you in the area that you have studied and use it to your advantage.

Do not belittle what you have, be it knowledge, skills, or abilities. What you have has the potential for multiplication once it is put to use. Work with what you have while striving to acquire the other things you desire. Seek to maximize the potential in what you have while you have it. Don't be like the child who missed the opportunity to play as he insisted on not going out to play with the ball that he already had because he did not get the toy he wanted.

Vision, Mission, and Values

There are some other internal drivers that should be considered in determining what you should do in moving forward. These also indicate what you should strive towards and represent the *why* as you move forward. These include your vision, mission, and values.

Values

Having lived for years, you would have internalized your experiences in the home, school, society, religious institutions, peer relations, culture, and other areas of life. These help to shape your values. Values represent the principles or standards of behavior and what you consider important or worth doing.

A conscientious individual will seek to be guided by his/her values in making decisions. In so doing, there will be some level of satisfaction and a personal sense of achievement and fulfillment in accomplishing things that matter to one. A person guided by values will also be able to secure his/her identity, being confident in doing what is important to him/her. Values are also useful in maintaining physical and mental health.

Living by your values is critical in going forward. Values represent that true north that provides the compass bearing for your life. Persons who are not living by their values are off course and need to be redirected. Persons who do not know their values are adrift and can end up anywhere in the sea of life.

What are the values that you have chosen to live by? Can you itemize them? How are they guiding you in the various spheres of your life? It should be noted that values are not specific to a single situation and can, therefore, be applied in a variety of settings. As you seek to go forward, it is necessary to spend time determining or reminding yourself of your values. You should then seek to determine the extent to which you are living in concert with the espoused values.

Where actions do not match values, there is incongruence. This will need to be addressed by revising the action or revisiting your values, if you choose not to continue to live with the conflictual situation. The latter state would not be healthy. Intentionally using values as a guide for action and ensuring congruence between actions and values is advised in going forward.

Vision and Mission

How do you see yourself in the next ten years? What do you see yourself doing? What would you have accomplished? How will you be feeling? What value would you have added to others' lives? These questions are seeking to understand your vision and mission.

Your vision represents what you see for yourself in the future, that is, your goals for the future. Your mission speaks to what you see as your purpose and how you aim to pursue that purpose.

Many persons, as they grew up, had a dream for their lives. They had something that they wanted to do or achieve. Over time, the desires would have been adjusted with some things removed, some things added, and other things refined or redefined. Some people now have a bucket list of experiences or achievements they hope to have or accomplish during their lifetime.

Another popular means of representing one's ideas for the future is using a vision board. This is a collage of images and words that depict one's dreams, ambitions, and goals intended to create a focal point to inspire or motivate one to work towards them.

Kudos if you have a vision board, a bucket list, or any other means to represent your dreams. This suggests that you have thought about going forward and have taken action towards accomplishing this.

It is hoped, however, that they are more than mere representations and have indeed been serving to propel actions. If this is not the case, those lists and boards must be revisited and repositioned for use. That is one area in which you need to go forward. Ideas are not worth much until they are acted upon.

Your vision and mission are central to who you are as a person, as you embody your dreams and goals. If you have not taken the time to outline these, you are encouraged to do so.

It is okay to dream. Yes, it is okay to have a dream. It is not too late to start dreaming. It is not too late to set goals. No, it is never too late to set out in search of your dreams. There are many examples of others who accomplished their dreams and significant successes later in life, some after significant setbacks.

Nelson Mandela became president at 76 years old after spending 27 years in jail. Nobel and Pulitzer Prize-winning author, Toni Morrison, wrote her first novel at age 40, winning her Pulitzer Prize at age 56. Ray Kroc spent his career as a salesman before buying McDonald's at age 52, which has grown into one of the world's biggest fast-food franchises. Anna Mary Robertson Moses, better known as Grandma Moses, began her prolific painting career at 78. Arianna Huffington founded her namesake news publication, The Huffington Post, at age 55. The lives of these and others show that one can have a meaningful and impactful life at any age. Do not let your current circumstances detract you from dreaming.

Start taking steps or continue to take steps in the direction of your goals and dreams. You are important, and what you desire is important. You might have given up your dreams in favor of helping others accomplish their goals and dreams. Remember that loving yourself is also the right thing to do. Going after your own dreams and goals is about loving yourself. Your dreams and goals can be the destinations as you go forward. Each win will be a rest stop along the way, going in the direction of your values.

Reflections and Notes

How have your perspectives been transformed based on the concepts that were highlighted in this chapter? What is your *why* that will guide you as you move forward? What steps do you need to take to clarify your *why* to help you move forward?

_____

_____

_____

_____

_____

_____

_____

_____

_____

_____

_____

_____

_____

_____

_____

ABOUT THE AUTHOR

Keshawna Salmon-Ferguson, PhD is committed to adding value to others through God-inspired words and actions. Her passion is for supporting and leading individuals and teams to discover, maximize, and work with their strengths while offering advanced strategies to achieve higher levels of performance and well-being as persons better understand themselves and are helped to deal with problem situations.

With postgraduate training in education and leadership, curriculum and instruction, counselling psychology, and more than 20 years' experience working with adolescents and adults in education and counselling practice, she has developed competence in propelling people forward as she meets them at the point of their needs. She is also a member of the John Maxwell certified team, further equipping her to train, speak, and coach.

The desire to support others in achieving their full potential has inspired her to launch Optim-Ed Professional Services, an organization that provides counselling, coaching, and educational services. She is also co-founder of the ARISE:

Support and Empowerment Ministries, a not-for-profit organization dedicated to supporting Ministers of Religion, their spouses, and children.

Dr. Salmon-Ferguson's impact and reach are international, working with persons across various regions and continents. She has been credited with facilitating transformation in individuals, teams, families, churches, and various groups through her writing, teaching, counselling, captivating presentations, and workshop sessions.

www.ingramcontent.com/pod-product-compliance
Lightning Source LLC
Chambersburg PA
CBHW071421090426
42737CB00011B/1533